W9-ACR-146

GAUGUIN

© THE BAKER & TAYLOR CO.

GAUGUIN

Watercolors, Pastels, Drawings

Jean Leymarie

SKIRA

RIZZOLI
NEW YORK

The text of this book was first published
in 1961 by Phoebus Verlag, Basel

This edition published in the United States of America in 1989 by

Rizzoli INTERNATIONAL PUBLICATIONS, INC.
597 Fifth Avenue/New York 10017

© 1989 by Editions d'Art Albert Skira S.A., Geneva

Translated from the French by Robert Allen

Printed in Switzerland

Library of Congress Cataloging-in-Publication Data

Leymarie, Jean.
   [Gauguin. English]
   Gauguin: watercolors, pastels, drawings / Jean Leymarie.
     p.   cm.
   Translation of: Gauguin.
   ISBN 0-8478-1050-X:
    1. Gauguin, Paul, 1848-1903—Catalogs.   I. Gauguin, Paul,
1848-1903. II. Title.
N6853.G34A4   1989
760'.092'4—dc 19

                            88-43447
                               CIP

TABLE OF GRAPHIC TECHNIQUES

Flora Tristan (1803–1844)

Paul Gauguin's grandmother.
Anonymous lithograph. Bibliothèque Nationale, Paris.

The very sound of Gauguin's name conjures up a world of colour, but we are not so apt to think of him as a draughtsman in the ordinary sense of the word. Actually, novel colour harmonies imply a correspondingly novel method of drawing and Gauguin, like Cézanne and Van Gogh, struggled indefatigably to create and master the form of his colour. Many of his drawings have been lost or destroyed. But his sketchbooks, though often dismembered, together with the illustrations in his numerous manuscripts and on many isolated sheets—not to mention his engravings—suffice to reveal an effort whose magnitude and originality have not received full recognition.

In *Avant et Après*, written in 1903 shortly before his death, Gauguin says: "What is drawing? Don't expect a lecture from me on that subject. A critic probably has a lot of things to say on paper with a pencil, thinking no doubt that that is how one can decide whether a man knows how to draw . . . I have never been able to draw properly, or use a paper-stump or a lump of bread. It always seems to me that something is missing: *the colour*." Though based, to use his own words, on "sharpness of outline," it is their colour that brings Gauguin's best drawings, like his paintings, to life. This album aims at offering a selection, both typical and varied, of Gauguin's production in this field.

Gauguin's life was so rich in contrasts that it was an obvious subject for literary exploitation and has indeed been so inordinately dramatized that we have formed a distorted picture of its true rhythm, which was slower and more austere. In Gauguin every metamorphosis involved a painful, mysterious uphill grind; it was not the soaring leap we are all too romantically apt to imagine. But he was an absolutist, at once arrogant and tortured; he wanted all or nothing. "I loathe half measures," he said. "I must have the whole lot. I cannot do it but I want to master it." And indeed nothing was vouchsafed him without a struggle—not even his tardy vocation for painting.

Paul Gauguin was born in Paris in 1848 but spent his childhood in Peru, "that wonderful land where it never rains," under the premonitory auspices of exotic magic. In 1865, when he was seventeen years old and already eager for a life of freedom and adventure in the open air, he went to sea and for six years sailed the South Atlantic as a pilot's apprentice, like Baudelaire and Manet at the same age. His father died in 1849 and his mother in 1867. When he got his discharge in 1871 his guardian, Gustave Arosa, a financier, placed him in a Paris stockbroker's office where he was soon making money. Through Arosa, who was also an enlightened connoisseur—he owned pictures by Delacroix, Corot, Courbet, Daumier, Jongkind and Pissarro—Gauguin became interested in painting to which he straightaway devoted all his free time. In 1873 he married Mette Gad, a pretty Danish society girl, who bore him five children in ten years of happy wedlock and material prosperity. But the demon of painting had already taken possession of him and his passion was aided and abetted by Emile Schuffenecker, who worked in the same office and became his closest friend. Gauguin's quick profits on the stock exchange placed him in a position to become a collector. He discovered the Impressionists at the very start of the movement, when they were most violently attacked, and bought a large number of their works which (together with drawings by Daumier and Degas and water-colours by Jongkind) he used for reference and inspiration. He also collected oriental rugs, Rouen pottery and Japanese prints. In 1876 a landscape of his—still reminiscent of Corot—was accepted by the Salon, and in the following year he took up sculpture, which satisfied his deep feeling for mass and volume.

It was at that time that he met Camille Pissarro, probably through Arosa who was a patron of the Impressionist leader. Pissarro, the moral conscience and artistic guide of his day, the heir to Corot's teachings, always ready to welcome a new departure, had already converted Cézanne. He appeared at just the right moment to encourage and direct Gauguin's work and soon obtained his admission, despite Monet's opposition, to the exhibitions held by the Impressionist group. During the summer vacation of 1879 Gauguin worked on the same motifs as Pissarro at Pontoise, where he returned in 1881 with Cézanne and Guillaumin. Pissarro probably gave him the very advice he later (when Gauguin was still with him) gave his son Lucien: the gist of it was to give his drawings a personal quality based rather on character than on virtuosity. "One must draw, and draw again... It is only by drawing often, drawing everything, drawing incessantly, that one day you are amazed to discover that you have found the way to render a thing with its own character... Little bits of sketches are not enough. You need them too, of course, to learn to see rapidly and render the overall character, but in order to get strong you must apply yourself seriously to large drawings with very *firm outlines*... Don't make pretty, clever little lines, but be simple and insist on the major lines that count in a face."

Self-Portraits
Side by Side
(Gauguin and Pissarro)

About 1883.
Charcoal and colour crayons.
31.5 × 49 cm.
Musée du Louvre, Paris.

The earliest of Gauguin's drawings still extant are a few pages from albums, a pencil portrait of Pissarro dated 1880, and innumerable studies of his wife and children. Of these we have chosen the watercolour of *Aline*, his favourite daughter, for its sensitive freshness and excellent rendering of the light. These works are still timid and conventional and reveal more diligence than real talent. Far from having to resist the facility condemned by his mentor because it is so often a pitfall for beginners, Gauguin had to overcome at the start his natural lack of talent. It was only his sincerity that taught him the clear, direct vision which he achieved the hard way. "To draw frankly," he said later, "means to be

Aline

About 1879-1880. Watercolour. 18.6 × 16.2 cm. Private Collection, Basel.

During ten years of happy wedlock and material prosperity Gauguin's pretty Danish wife Mette bore him five children—four boys and a girl. This daughter, who was the second eldest, was born on Christmas Day 1877. She was christened Aline after Gauguin's mother and was his favourite. It was for her that, in Tahiti in 1893, he wrote his still unpublished *Cahier pour Aline* now in the Bibliothèque d'Art et d'Archéologie, Paris. In these "scattered notes" he endeavoured to give an unembellished account of his experience as man and artist. This darling daughter was only twenty years old when she was carried off by pneu-

monia in 1897. The cruel blow wrung from Gauguin—in his last letter to his wife, which never received an answer—the dreadful cry: "I have lost my daughter, I no longer love God."

When Gauguin began to draw, as an amateur, under the guidance of Pissarro, he quite naturally took his wife and children as his first models. Most of those family sketches were hoarded by Mette and are today in Danish collections.

This watercolour, still awkward but showing great sensibility, belonged to the Spanish sculptor and ceramist Paco (Francisco) Durrio (1876-1940), a devoted pupil and admirer of Gauguin from whom he bought some paintings and a large number of drawings and prints. It is very probably a portrait of Aline for it closely resembles the three pencil sketches done slightly earlier.

honest with oneself." If his career started late and developed slowly, he had the immense advantage of entering into immediate contact with the living art of his day and escaping the dangers of the academic routine he ridiculed in his *Racontars de Rapin*. "To know how to draw does not mean to draw well. Let's examine the famous science of draughtsmanship we hear so much about. Every *Prix de Rome* has that science at his finger-tips; so have the competitors who come in last... It is a science they acquire easily, without the slightest effort, while spending their time in beer-halls and brothels."

Gauguin's steady progress, his tenacity, and his thorough, personal study of the great artists of the previous generation, from Courbet to Monet and Renoir, awakened interest in him. In 1881 Huysmans praised in the warmest terms his famous *Study of the Nude* (Ny Carlsberg Glyptotek, Copenhagen), "a fearless and authentic work of art," uncompromisingly realistic and with firm outlines. In 1882 Gauguin helped Caillebotte to prepare the seventh Impressionist exhibition to which he contributed, among other works, a number of pastels. This is a medium he was fond of employing, especially in his early period, first for studies of heads of a slightly cloying sweetness and later for other subjects, often applying the coloured chalks over a black chalk or charcoal drawing (like the *Woman Bather in Brittany*). The pastel, or "dry colouring method," is a French invention that dates back to Jean Fouquet and was developed by the Clouets. It came into fashion in the eighteenth century, for its gossamer lightness and liveliness suited the sensibility of the period; but even so it was still considered a second-rate art practised only by specialists and for portraits. After 1880 Manet and Degas, the first because of his paralysed hand, the second on account of his bad eyesight, brought pastel back to favour and used practically no other medium. By introducing a new style and a new technique they brilliantly extended its potentialities. Gauguin learnt to use pastel from

Woman Bather in Brittany

1886. Black chalk and pastel. 57.3 × 34.7 cm.
Signed, lower left: P. Gauguin.
The Art Institute of Chicago.

During his first stay at Pont-Aven, from June to November 1886, Gauguin did several drawings of Breton women in local costume and this important nude—in which the treatment is still timid and naturalistic—stooping apprehensively towards the water, with one hand on her knee and the other on the rocky bank.

As usual with Gauguin, the same motif, in the same typical posture, was later repeated several times in different media. Thus we find it in an oil, *Two Girls Bathing*, dated 1887 (National Museum of Fine Arts, Buenos Aires); on a design for a fan in pastel, also dated 1887, where the figure is cut off waist-high by the shape of the fan; on a ceramic vase of 1888; and finally, reversed, in *Breton Girls Bathing*, one of the zincographs executed in 1889.

Gauguin no doubt got the idea from Degas with whom he was in contact at the time and who had shown, at the eighth and last Impressionist exhibition in May and June 1886, his famous "series of female nudes bathing, washing, drying themselves, doing their hair and having it done." This theme of bathers was resumed by Gauguin, now master of his own personal style, during his second, decisive stay at Pont-Aven in June and July 1888. On July 8 he wrote to Schuffenecker: "I have done a few nudes that you will be satisfied with. And they are not at all Degas."

Pissarro who employed it chiefly for the decorative works he was forced to produce in large numbers to make a living.

In 1883 Gauguin felt he was a real artist and no longer an amateur ("The only amateurs," Manet told him shortly before his death, "are the people who paint badly"). Sure at last of his vocation, he took the decisive step of giving up business and a regular job and devoting all his time to his art. Though less sudden than legend has it and probably speeded up by the economic crisis prevailing at the time, this decision was none the less heroic for it pledged Gauguin's entire future. He was thirty-five years old when he entered upon a life of trials which he could not foresee but accepted without flinching—the life of an accursed artist, an outcast from society, crowned by genius only at the price of solitude and destitution.

His first step was to follow Pissarro's example and move to Rouen because he imagined it would be cheaper to live in a provincial town and hoped, naïvely, that the rich merchants there would buy his pictures. But he was speedily disillusioned. His savings were soon spent and Mette, finding herself unable to cope with what she called her husband's lunacy, lost her nerve and took refuge with her family in Denmark in October 1884. Paul followed her there in November, having accepted the Scandinavian agency of a Roubaix tarpaulin manufacturer. Though he worked hard he did not make a success of the venture. For the quondam clever financier, despite the new mirages that constantly allured him, the future was to hold nothing but disappointment in money matters for he was entirely obsessed by painting. "Here more than ever I am tormented by art and neither money worries nor business projects can take my mind off it," he wrote to Schuffenecker on January 14, 1885, a few weeks after reaching Denmark.

In this very important letter, which would be worth quoting in full, he already set forth in clear terms the essentials of his future aesthetic creed. Feeling takes precedence over thought, but thought is more important than sight; "all five senses reach *the brain direct*"; the expression should be simple: "a great emotion can be translated immediately; dream over it and look for its simplest form"; lines and colours have a magic power; "I infer that there are noble lines, false lines, etc.; a straight line expresses infinity, a curve limits creation, not to mention the portentous significance of numbers. Some tones are noble, others common; some harmonies are quiet and cheering, others excite you by their boldness . . . The further I go, the more I feel sure that thoughts can be expressed by something quite different from literature."

These were indeed strange preoccupations in the hidebound bourgeois environment of Copenhagen into which he had been transplanted and where he was the object of a curiosity that soon turned to contempt. It was not long before Gauguin had had enough of the bickering of the Danes, whom his manners shocked just as much as his pictures, and the hostility of his in-laws who tried to take his wife away from him. In June or July 1885 he returned to Paris with his son Clovis. The legend tends to simplify a complex drama of married life by saying that he abandoned his family. Actually it was merely a separation which could hardly be helped. The bitter tone of his letters proves that—right up to his second stay in Tahiti—he hoped it would be only temporary. In fact, he was never to live with his wife again. "We have no reason to regret it," his son Pola said; "for left to his own devices, Gauguin was able to devote himself entirely to his art in a spirit of complete physical and moral freedom."

During the unhappy but fruitful months he spent in Denmark, Gauguin not only worked out the theoretical foundations of his art but also produced a number of pictures that break away from Impressionism and proclaim a personal vision of his own. Space is contracted, line strongly stressed. "Line," he observed on May 24, 1885, speaking of Delacroix, "is a means of stressing an idea." His colours, blended rather than divided, with delicate concords rather than strident discords, produce a dreamy harmony. As usual he did a lot of drawings, especially of his children, for he had a presentiment that he was soon to leave them. The almost unknown design for a fan in gouache, *Study after Cézanne*, reproduced here, is inscribed "Copenhague 1885." It is the luminous, nobly rhythmic interpretation of a landscape painted by Cézanne shortly before, and whose monumental grandeur is too overpowering for the merely ornamental scope of a fan. We know from Gauguin himself that he owned as many as twelve pictures by Cézanne. Studied in every detail, they had a decisive influence on his artistic schooling, teaching him depth and weight of colour and the rhythmic arrangement of the picture plane.

At that time the fashion for fans, whether painted or adorned with poems, coincided with the universal craze for Japanese art and lore. The fourth Impressionist exhibition in April-May 1879 (where Gauguin showed a piece of sculpture for the first time) had a whole room full of fans by Degas, Pissarro, Berthe Morisot and Marie Bracquemond. Some were actually mounted and put to practical use; but the majority, though given the right shape, were left in the design stage and served as a pretext for exquisite refinements of colour. To earn a living and make his name known to the general public, Pissarro spent a lot of time on this speciality and the catalogue of his œuvre mentions no less than fifty-six fans, mostly produced about 1885. Several documents on Gauguin, and in particular the lists contained in his notebooks, prove that he too executed a large number, most of which he presented to friends or admirers. A dozen or so are still extant, the majority in gouache (like those by Degas and Pissarro), some in watercolours, and a very few in pastels. The one reproduced here was done in Martinique.

After a mysterious journey to Dieppe and London, Gauguin spent a miserable winter in Paris, where at one time he was reduced to such straits that he had to work as a bill-poster to earn a living

Study for a Fan
after Cézanne

*1885. Gouache. 27.9 × 55.5 cm. Inscribed, lower
left: dédié à M. Pietro Krohn / P. Gauguin /
Copenhague 1885.*
Ny Carlsberg Glyptotek, Copenhagen.

Executed during Gauguin's stay in Copenhagen (November 1884 to June or July 1885) after a canvas by Cézanne (*Mountains at L'Estaque*, about 1883-1885, National Museum of Wales, Cardiff). Cézanne and Gauguin were brought together by Pissarro at Pontoise in the summer of 1881. Gauguin was one of the first and most ardent admirers of Cézanne, whose work had a decisive influence on his artistic development. The collection of pictures formed during his years as a banker before 1883, which was left to his wife in Denmark and acquired by his brother-in-law Edvard Brandes, included twelve Cézannes (letter to Emmanuel Bibesco, undated, Tahiti, July 1900). Speaking of one

of them, he writes: "The Cézanne you ask me about is an exceptional pearl... I value it like the apple of my eye and, unless absolutely compelled, I will part with it only after my last shirt" (letter to Emile Schuffenecker, Pont-Aven, June 1888). The "Cézanne with red roofs" which he tried to recover in February 1894, in exchange for one of his own canvases, may be the one here referred to (letter to his wife, Paris, February 5, 1894). On January 14, 1885, he wrote to Schuffenecker from Copenhagen: "Look at the much misunderstood Cézanne. His is the essentially mystical nature of the Oriental (his face resembles that of a wise man of the East). The form he prefers has the mystery and the heavy stillness of a man lying down to dream; his colour is grave like the character of the Orientals. A man of the South, he spends whole days on the tops of mountains reading Virgil and gazing at the sky. So his horizons are lofty, his blues very intense, and his reds have an astonishing vibrancy."

More will be said about fan painting in the commentary on another fan (page 18).

Study for a Fan
(Landscape on Martinique)

1887. Gouache. 12 × 42 cm. Signed, lower left:
P. Gauguin.
Private Collection, Basel.

Several of the motifs treated during Gauguin's stay on Martinique in the summer of 1887 have been freely combined here in a charming decorative synthesis.

The vogue for fans, to which even poets pandered, spread among the Impressionist and Post-Impressionist painters as a result of the mania for Japanese art and lore. At the fourth Impressionist exhibition in April-May 1879, a whole room was filled with fans by Degas, Pissarro, Berthe Morisot and Marie Bracquemond. Some were actually mounted and used, but many were left as simple fan-shaped sketches of exquisite refinement but of no practical utility. Pissarro, to earn a living and bring his name before the public, cultivated this genre systematically, especially about 1885, and the catalogue of his œuvre includes no fewer than fifty-six fans.

Known documents on Gauguin and especially, for his pre-Tahitian period, the list included in *Le Carnet de Paul Gauguin* (published by René Huyghe in 1952) mention the existence of several fans, most of which he presented to his friends and admirers. For these little works he employed sometimes gouache (like Degas), sometimes watercolour, more seldom pastel.

Another of Gauguin's fans (*Study for a Fan after Cézanne*) is reproduced on page 17.

and take care of his sick child. Those difficulties, far from disheartening him, strengthened his purpose and made him still more obstinate in following the path he had chosen. In May 1886, at the eighth and last Impressionist exhibition, he showed no less than nineteen canvases, which Félix Fénéon praised for their original density, four-square solidity, and the "muted harmony" of rust-reds and greens. The most controversial picture in the exhibition was Seurat's *Sunday Afternoon on the Island of La Grande Jatte*, which showed Gauguin what his experiments still lacked, namely colour; and he guessed its potentialities at once. He too, like Lautrec, Van Gogh and, later, Matisse and Kandinsky, had his pointillist phase, but it was short-lived and violently repudiated. Félix Bracquemond, the engraver, a friend of Degas and the discoverer of Hokusai, bought one of Gauguin's canvases. He also introduced him to the ceramist Ernest Chaplet, "as great an artist as the Chinese," with the idea that they might work together.

In June 1886 Gauguin went to Pont-Aven, a small town in the department of Finistère already well known to painters for its cheapness and beautiful scenery, and remained there till November at the Gloanec Inn. This first stay in Brittany, though disregarded by many students of Gauguin, was not without its importance, particularly in the field of graphic art with which we are concerned here. "I do a lot of sketches," he wrote to his wife shortly after his arrival; and on the point of returning to Paris: "I am packing up my work. A lot of sketches." In accordance with the method then in vogue, Gauguin copied from nature in summer the motifs—in the literal sense of the word—which he utilized in his studio during the winter. Moreover, at each new stage and in each new country he needed what he called "a period of incubation," which he spent chiefly observing and drawing. This process became a regular habit of his.

The date of four very finished, large-size studies in charcoal, black chalk and pastel—one dedicated to his new comrade Charles

Laval—was long uncertain. Merete Bodelsen has demonstrated that they must be attributed beyond question to this first stay in Brittany. Three of them portray, in naïve, graceful postures reminiscent of Courbet, peasant women in local costume, one seated (Art Institute of Chicago), the other two standing viewed respectively from side and rear (Glasgow Art Gallery). The last and most important of the four is the nude figure of a *Woman Bather* (Art Institute of Chicago), looking apprehensively at the water with one hand resting on her knee and the other on the steep bank. Although the outline that poetically encloses the musing figure is already deliberately stressed, the treatment is still naturalistic and inspired by Degas's recently shown "series of female nudes bathing." But the girl's hesitant—one might even say, suspended—pose is hit off so perfectly, and is so consonant with the artist's sensibility, that we find it repeated several times in the most diverse media: in 1887 in an oil painting and a pastel design for a fan; in 1888 on a ceramic vase (which, in turn, was introduced in a still life of the same year); and finally in a zincograph in 1889. This peculiar economy in the choice of motifs, which once fixed were continually repeated, was typical of Gauguin and reveals both his difficulties as a creative artist and his talent for composition; for him invention counted less than decorative arrangement and rhythm.

Back in Paris, Gauguin devoted practically all his time to designing ceramics for Chaplet, taking as his models the motifs he had recently drawn in Brittany. The necessity of engraving in clay a sharp line heightened with gold caused him to simplify his contours, which tended away from realism and the delicate chiaroscuro of charcoal towards ornamental stylization. Thus ceramic work modified his drawing technique and led him to the "cloisonnism" that typified his later style. During that same winter, which is a very important link in his artistic development, Gauguin drew away from Pissarro and approached Degas; he also met Vincent van Gogh with whom he struck up a strange friendship.

The year 1886 is a definite turning point in the history of art. It saw the publication of Rimbaud's *Illuminations*, Van Gogh's arrival in Paris, Gauguin's first stay in Brittany, Lautrec's first steps, and the revelation of Seurat. It sanctioned the scission of the Impressionists and the birth of a new movement for which the poet Jean Moréas, in his manifesto published in the *Figaro* of September 18, proposed the name of Symbolism, "as the only one capable of giving a reasonable definition of the present trend of the creative spirit in art." Its essential formula, valid in all spheres, was "to clothe an idea in a visible form." Painters no longer aimed at directly depicting the outer world but at rendering their inner dreams by symbolic allusion and the luxuriant garb of decorative form. Line and colour developed their powers of expression and became the "abstract" equivalents of sensation. This trend was followed by all artists, whether the path they chose was mystical or scientific.

In April 1887, after being tormented in Paris by poverty and obsessed by the mirage of far-off lands, Gauguin sailed with Charles Laval for Panama where he planned to live "like a savage." Cruel disappointment awaited them, however, and after two months they went on to Martinique which they found "a paradise compared with the isthmus." They were fascinated by the scenery and the creole life, which they could not, however, enjoy to the full because they were so exhausted by sickness and fever that they had to return to Europe in November. Nonetheless, Gauguin himself said the voyage was "a decisive experience" on the human and artistic level for it proved the existence of the "paradise" that obsessed him. Under the burning sky of Martinique his vision became broadened and refined, his line firmer and more supple, his colour freer and deeper. "I am bringing back a dozen canvases, including four with figures that are far better than those of my Pont-Aven period," he wrote to Schuffenecker, "good old Schuff," who welcomed and harboured him on his return to Paris.

He also had a quantity of drawings, rapid sketches of natives in motion, decorative syntheses of the country and its people, the moving profile of a *Negress* (Rijksmuseum Vincent van Gogh, Amsterdam) viewed from close-up. This pastel and several oils from Martinique were bought by Vincent van Gogh's brother Theo at the exhibition of Gauguin's work which he organized in January 1888 in the Boussod and Valadon Gallery on the Boulevard Montmartre. Vincent admired them before leaving for Arles in February.

In that same month Gauguin went back to Pont-Aven. It was during this second stay in Brittany that he worked out his personal style. He was spellbound by that remote, archaic land whose primitiveness and melancholy harmonized with his soul and art. "When my clogs," he said, "strike against this granite ground I hear the dull, muffled, yet strong tone I want to put in my pictures." And in fact it is less to its intensity than to its overtones that his colour owes its magic. Once again he took *Bathers* as his theme, but now more freely and expressively than in 1886.

Study of Native Women

1887. Watercolour. 20.9 × 26.8 cm.
Private Collection, Basel.

After the cruel disappointment suffered at Panama, Gauguin and his comrade Charles Laval stayed on Martinique, in the West Indies, from June to October 1887.

There Gauguin was captivated not only by the luxuriant vegetation but also by the charm of the natives, the beauty of their colourful costumes, their noble carriage and bearing. He tried to jot down to the life their graceful, lively silhouettes in a great variety of postures. This rapid, agile sketch shows how supple his drawing has now become.

For other Martinique studies of an entirely different type, the reader is referred to the illustrations on the following pages.

24

Women of Martinique

1887. Pastel. 48.5 × 64 cm.
Signed, lower right: PG.
Private Collection, Paris.

Head of a Negress

1887. Pastel. 36 × 27 cm. Signed, upper left:
P. Gauguin.
Rijksmuseum Vincent van Gogh, Amsterdam.

Vincent van Gogh's brother Theo was manager of the small art gallery on the Boulevard Montmartre, one of Messrs. Goupil's three establishments, where he courageously attempted to show the Impressionists and their successors. In January 1888 he held a Gauguin exhibition, which was not a success. For himself he bought a number of works done on Martinique, including this remarkable pastel.

Vincent admired them before leaving for Arles in February 1888 and later exchanged a canvas of his own for one of Gauguin's Martinique pictures. In May he wrote to Emile Bernard: "Oh! How right you are to think of Gauguin! Those negresses of his are sublime poems, and everything from his hand is gentle, sad, wonderful. People do not understand him yet and he suffers deeply because, like other real poets, he does not sell."

Most of the paintings and drawings done on Martinique are decorative compositions enlivened by graceful silhouettes. But here we have a touching portrait of an individual face viewed in profile from close up and of a general human type.

The supple, unbroken line he had first adopted in the West Indies he now used to limn adolescent nudes and developed boldly in *Breton Girls Dancing*, the fine preliminary pastel for which is reproduced here (Rijksmuseum Vincent van Gogh, Amsterdam); it is one of Gauguin's few studies of movement, for he preferred motionless, pensive postures. In *Avant et Après* we find this advice: "Everything in your work should breathe calm and peace of mind. So avoid figures in motion; they must all be in a state of repose." He wrote to Schuffenecker on July 8, 1888: "I have just done a few *nudes* you will like. And they're not at all Degas. The last... quite Japanese, by a savage from Peru." His transformation was accelerated by the arrival of Emile Bernard; on August 14 he confided to Schuffenecker his famous formula: "Art is an abstraction; derive that abstraction from nature by dreaming before her."

In September he painted *Jacob Wrestling with the Angel* (National Gallery of Scotland, Edinburgh). This revolutionary masterpiece stated, under the combined influence of Japanese woodcuts, medieval stained-glass windows, French popular prints, and the Italian Primitives, the new principles of *Cloisonnism* and *Synthetism*—division of the picture plane into areas of a single colour; arbitrary choice of unmodulated colours; simplification of objects into arabesques. The non-illusionistic composition, with neither shadows, modelling or skyline, is based on the rhythmic vibration of the contours that maintain the coloured planes. Hence the fundamental law, which was formulated in *Avant et Après* and is vindicated here: "Pay attention to the silhouette of each object; a clear outline is the prerogative of a hand that is not paralysed by a faltering will."

The most striking demonstration of this principle is found in the exemplary drawing *L'Arlésienne* (M.H. de Young Memorial Museum, San Francisco), which Gauguin gave Van Gogh when he stayed with him in Provence from the end of October to Christmas of 1888. At once symbol and portrait, classically perfect

Breton Girls Dancing

1888. Pastel. 24.2 × 41 cm.
Rijksmuseum Vincent van Gogh, Amsterdam.

A study for (or after) the picture dated 1888, formerly in the Vollard Collection (now in the Mellon Collection, Upperville, Virginia), which appeared as No. 36 under the title *Round Dance in the Hay* in the famous exhibition held in the Café Volpini in Paris in connection with the 1889 World's Fair; it later adorned the dining-room of Marie Henry's inn at Le Pouldu. The three little peasant girls, here only visible from the waist up, are dancing in clogs on the new-mown hay outside the Breton village of Pont-Aven. Movement studies are rather rare in Gauguin who delighted in motionless, dreamy poses, and the traditional round dance develops slowly towards an ultimate suspense. The girls' faces, which are closer together in the pastel than in the oil, are imbued with the pure, naïve grace Gauguin sought in Brittany. He has succeeded in varying their profiles, making the most of the decorative aspects of coif and costume, and turning the picturesque into poetry. The same happy combination of order and sentiment is to be found in another picture painted at that time, *Four Breton Women Dancing* (Neue Pinakothek, Munich).

in its nobility of pose and costume, it is done in charcoal without any heightening; a medium that Redon, who, like Corot, adopted it for its mystery and gravity, called the "black pastel which only real feeling can make the best of." Gauguin's watercolours of *Washerwomen at Arles*, "with their elegant headdress, their Grecian beauty, their shawls that form folds like the Primitives," their flat silhouettes in bright colours without any shadows, bear witness to the influence of Japanese prints then at its height. "Look at the Japanese who draw so admirably," he wrote to Emile Bernard, "and you will see life in the open air and in the sun without any shadows... Shadows are the sun's *trompe-l'œil*, so I am inclined to suppress them."

Provence was Van Gogh's Japan and there since the month of March 1888, like Gauguin in Brittany, he had directed all his efforts towards obtaining "colours like those in stained-glass windows and a drawing with firm lines." When the two painters

L'Arlésienne

1888 (November). Charcoal. 56 × 48.4 cm. Inscribed, upper right: l'œil moins à côté du nez / Arête vive / à la [main?] narine. *M.H. de Young Memorial Museum, San Francisco.*

When Gauguin arrived at Arles on the evening of October 23, 1888, he stopped at the *Night Café* Van Gogh had depicted the previous month in a fascinating, dramatic picture (Yale University Art Gallery, New Haven) that had deeply impressed him. In November Gauguin produced his own version, *At the Café (Mme Ginoux)* (Pushkin Museum, Moscow), which differs in conception from Van Gogh's picture. It shows us, in the foreground, the figure of a woman with her elbow leaning on a marble-topped table. There is a sketch of the entire composition in a letter from Gauguin to Emile Bernard. This charcoal drawing is a preliminary sketch for the female figure.

The model was Madame Ginoux whose husband owned the café; she also sat for Van Gogh's famous *Arlésienne* of which there are two versions: a rougher one in the Louvre and a more finished one in the Metropolitan Museum of Art, New York. In all probability Gauguin drew Madame Ginoux while Vincent was painting her, "dashing off her portrait in an hour," as he wrote to Theo. In the two pictures the posture and costume are identical, but viewed from different angles. Gustave Coquiot, who compiled the recollections of the Ginoux couple and published the first of the four friendly letters Vincent wrote them from Saint-Rémy and Auvers, tells how the two painters "set a trap to make Madame Ginoux sit to them by inviting her for coffee."

Gauguin gave his drawing to Van Gogh who was inspired by it to do four new versions of the *Arlésienne* at Saint-Rémy. One of these he sent to Gauguin, then at Le Pouldu, who admired it and wrote to thank him in June 1890. Vincent replied at once: "It gives me enormous pleasure that you say the portrait of the Arlésienne, based entirely on your drawing, pleased you. I tried to be respectfully true to your drawing while taking the liberty to interpret it by means of a colour in keeping with the sober character and the style of the drawing in question. It is a synthesis of *Arlésiennes*, if you like; since syntheses of *Arlésiennes* are rare, accept this one as your work and mine, a résumé of the months we worked together."

joined forces the first result was mutual enthusiasm. But, as Gauguin said later, "between two people, him and me, one all volcano and the other boiling too, but inwardly, there was a struggle of some sort brewing." Vincent was concerned with human passions and modelled forms, while Gauguin sought abstract beauty and flat forms; the latter all imagination, the former at grips with reality. This aesthetic divergence concealed "a profound human cleavage" (Artaud) and the crisis was bound to come violently to a head. Years later Gauguin drew the following conclusion from that dramatic and fruitful clash: "Without the public's noticing anything, two men did a colossal job which was useful to them both. And perhaps for others too. Some things bear their fruit." Van Gogh, whose nordic heritage still kept him liege to angular, broken drawing, received from Gauguin a taste for arabesques and for linear stylization which he developed further at Saint-Rémy when he copied his friend's *Arlésienne*. In return he imparted to Gauguin a little of his mystic fire and gave him the decisive impulse which drew forth the power that till then had remained dormant.

The invaluable *Carnet de Paul Gauguin* published in 1952 deals exclusively with that all-important year 1888 and contains sketches done in Brittany and Provence. The difference between the two groups can be seen at a glance, not so much in their style as in the spirit that imbues it. At that time Gauguin did a lot of animal drawings and thick-set, placid cows are typical of the Breton series. Rather surprisingly a dozen sheets done at Arles—unquestionably the best of the whole album—are devoted to the wild animals with which Delacroix had passionately identified himself. "Delacroix's drawing," Gauguin noted in 1885, "always reminds me of a tiger's strong, supple movements." After Arles, as René Huyghe says in his introduction to the *Carnet*, "a new tone, evident in the whiplash arabesques and the brilliant colouring, gives Gauguin's most static and hieratic scenes a sort of inner fire which is the fascination—now apparent for the first time—of his genius."

Washerwomen at Arles

1888. Watercolour on silk. 10.1 × 20.3 cm.
Signed, lower right: P. Gauguin.
Formerly Arthur Sachs Collection.

In November 1888 Van Gogh wrote to his brother Theo: "Gauguin is working hard ... just now he is doing landscapes and a good canvas of washerwomen, very good indeed in my opinion."

Our watercolour corresponds to the central portion of an oil painting of Arles washerwomen now in Mr. and Mrs. William S. Paley's collection in New York. Besides a more extensive landscape, the painting has in the foreground to the left two little girls' heads viewed from three-quarters and cut off by the frame, and at the far right, another washerwoman for which there is a separate pencil study on page 16 of *Le Carnet de Paul Gauguin*. The clearly drawn outlines, the flat silhouettes blocked out in colours without a trace of shadows bear witness to the influence of Japanese prints which was particularly strong at that time. Gauguin explains it in a letter to Emile Bernard in which he also stresses the beauty of the women of Arles and their costumes. "You argue with Laval about shadows and ask me if I ever give them a thought. As far as they serve to explain light, yes. Look at the Japanese who draw admirably and you will see life out of doors in the sun without any shadows ... It's curious, here Vincent feels bound to paint like Daumier while what I see instead is coloured Puvis mixed with Japan. The women here have an elegant head-dress and Greek beauty. Their shawls form folds like the primitives ..." (undated letter, Arles, November 1888).

During a short stay in Paris on his way back to Pont-Aven Gauguin did a set of eleven zincographs—the process resembles lithography, but with zinc as a base instead of stone—in which the chief motifs of Arles, Martinique and Brittany are decoratively stylized. They were printed on pale yellow paper and some proofs were heightened with watercolours. During the 1889 World's Fair the whole set was exhibited at the show held by the Impressionist and Synthetist group in the Café Volpini where Gauguin's pupils from Pont-Aven gathered round their master. The show was not a success as far as the general public was concerned, but it had a decisive influence on the formation of the Nabis who acknowledged Gauguin as the "undisputed leader" of the new movement (Maurice Denis). It is worth noting that in addition to the zincographs he also exhibited fourteen oils, two pastels and one watercolour.

Manao Tupapau
(Spirit of the Dead Watching)

About 1894. Woodcut partly coloured. 22.3 × 52.7 cm. Central detail taken over in Noa Noa, *page 75. The Art Institute of Chicago.*

Paul Gauguin
Les Cigales et les fourmie

The Cicadas and the Ants
(Memory of Martinique)

About 1889. Zincograph. 22.2 × 29.3 cm.
Department of Prints and Drawings,
The Royal Museum of Fine Arts, Copenhagen.

The Breton Eve

1889. Watercolour and pastel. 33.7 × 31.8 cm. Signed and dated, lower right: P. Gauguin 89. *Marion Koogler McNay Institute, San Antonio, Texas.*

At the exhibition organized by the Impressionist and Synthetist Group in the Café des Arts (Café Volpini), Place du Champ-de-Mars, Paris, in summer 1889 on the occasion of the World's Fair, No. 42 was a watercolour by Gauguin entitled "Eve"—probably the one reproduced here. Seated motionless on the ground with knees drawn up and her head in her hands, she leans against the trunk of a tree on which the serpent is coiled.

The sheet exhibited in the Café Volpini bore this inscription in pidgin French: "Pas écouter li...li menteur" (Not listen him... him liar). Reporting on the show in *Art et Critique* of November 9, 1889, Jules Antoine asks ironically: "On what document does Mr. Gauguin base his assumption that Eve spoke pidgin French?" To which the artist retorted, in a letter to Emile Bernard: "What an idiotic article!... it appears that Eve didn't speak pidgin French but, my God! what language did they speak, she and the serpent?" (undated, Le Pouldu, November 1889.)

This strange, dejected, naked woman, Gauguin's first woeful embodiment of Eve —so different from the others we shall see later—reappears symbolically more than once in his paintings, drawings, engravings and sculptures, as will be stressed in the commentary on *Nirvana (Meyer de Haan)*. Marked by the passage of time, but still in the same typical posture, she is the first figure to the left—representing old age—in the large composition of 1897, *Whence Come We? What Are We? Whither Go We?* (Museum of Fine Arts, Boston).

Downcast by the failure of a show on which he had placed all his hopes, Gauguin went back to Pont-Aven and from there to the lonely seaside village of Le Pouldu. His name is in the visitors' book of the inn kept there by Marie Henry, called Marie Poupée, from October 2, 1889, to November 7, 1890. At Le Pouldu his loyal and devoted disciple, the Dutch painter Meyer de Haan, shared his life and paid for both of them. Gauguin did several portraits, both painted and sculptured, of his strange comrade. He was the model for the hallucinated mask of a buddhistic idol that stands out against a background of writing female figures in *Nirvana*. This mysterious, poignant composition was executed at the time when Gauguin, under the impact of the oriental pavilions at the World's Fair of 1889, was deeply interested in Khmer art and Hindu thought. He was now entirely master of his style and technique and in November 1889 finished the *Yellow Christ* in which he achieved what he termed "the synthesis of form and colour while considering only the dominant." The form, deliberately crude and naïve, is copied from the wooden statues in Breton representations of the Crucifixion, while the rich dominant autumnal yellow renders the feeling of "resigned suffering" which imbued the artist at the time. This picture, undoubtedly the most significant work of Gauguin's Breton period, was prepared by a pencil study and a general sketch in watercolours. The same resignation is expressed in the sorrowful, dispirited figure of the

Meyer de Haan (Nirvana)

About 1890. Gouache and turpentine on silk. 20 × 28 cm. Signed, lower centre, on the hand: Gauguin. Inscribed, lower right: Nirvana.
Wadsworth Atheneum, Hartford, Connecticut.

The Dutch painter Jacob Meyer de Haan (1852-1895), son of a rich Amsterdam industrialist, had a monthly allowance which enabled him to devote all his time to his art. Pissarro recommended him to Gauguin whose enthusiastic and devoted admirer he became. He shared Gauguin's life at Pont-Aven and particularly at Le Pouldu where his money paid the costs of both. Under Gauguin's influence he painted landscapes, still lifes and portraits. Among the latter was one of the innkeeper Marie Henry which Gauguin greatly admired and for which he made a frame. "De Haan is getting on wonderfully here," he wrote to Emile Bernard in October 1889. De Haan was to have gone to the South Seas with Gauguin but his family dissuaded him on account of his health—he was ill and crippled—and kept him in Holland where he died shortly after. To Marie Henry, who had made Gauguin extremely jealous by becoming his mistress, De Haan bequeathed all his Breton works which, though not very numerous, were of excellent quality.

Gauguin was fascinated by his friend's strange face and deformed body, and painted him several times. Extant are a portrait in oils dated 1889 and a lifesize sculpture of the same period (National Gallery, Ottawa). The memory of Meyer de Haan still haunted Gauguin during his second stay in Tahiti, as witnessed by a woodcut, *Souvenir de Meyer de Haan*, and pursued him even as far as the Marquesas where Meyer de Haan's hallucinating, exhausted figure stands guard in the background of *Contes Barbares* of 1902 (Museum Folkwang, Essen). In our picture De Haan stands out against the mysterious, interlocked female figures like some sort of Buddhist divinity sunk in Nirvana (whence the inscription). It was painted soon after Gauguin sustained the impact of the Oriental pavilions at the Paris World's Fair of 1889.

The two naked figures in the background, whose faces are illuminated by a glare of footlights inspired perhaps by Degas's dancers, were the subject of a washed drawing entitled *Aux Roches Noires* used as frontispiece for the catalogue of the exhibition held in the Café Volpini in 1889. It was repeated on the cover of the album of drawings *Documents Tahiti, 1891-1892-1893* and in a woodcut executed during Gauguin's second stay in Tahiti, one proof of which was pasted on page 186 of the manuscript of *Noa Noa*. The figure on the left appears by itself several times in Gauguin's work; that on the right was the subject of a washed pen drawing, and of an oil of 1889, *Ondine* (Cleveland Museum of Art); and a woodcarving of 1890.

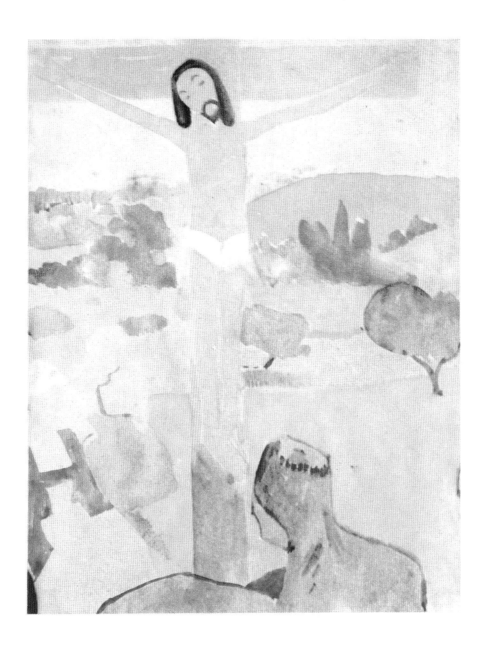

The Yellow Christ

1889. Watercolour. 15.2 × 12.1 cm.
Formerly Mrs. Gilbert W. Chapman Collection.

An overall sketch for the famous masterpiece of the same title (Albright-Knox Art Gallery, Buffalo, New York), which, commenced no doubt at Pont-Aven and finished at Le Pouldu in autumn 1889, is one of the highlights of Gauguin's Breton period. The general effect of the composition is perfectly suggested, with its values of flat space and symbolic colour, its "decorative" and "synthetic" harmony. Lacking are the details of the figures and, in the landscape, the architectural elements—houses nestling among the trees and a dry stone wall with human silhouettes. There is a pencil study for the figure of Christ alone, which looks as if it had been directly inspired by an "ivory-coloured" wooden crucifix still to be seen in the little chapel of Trémalo near Pont-Aven. "When you open the great door on a sunny day this Christ becomes indisputably yellow, especially as it stands out against a wall washed in bluish white, and beneath a wooden vault uncompromisingly blue." *The Yellow Christ* reappears in the background of a *Self-Portrait* of Gauguin (1889-1890) in the former Maurice Denis Collection. Though not a believer, Gauguin succeeded in rendering the popular, primitive religious spirit of Brittany, and in his painful struggle for art's sake he found strength in the example of Christ. Autumnal melancholy provides the rich keynote of the colour scheme and harmonizes with the impression of "resigned suffering" which, as Gauguin himself said, he felt and put into his work.

Breton Eve which differs so entirely from the pictures of Eve Gauguin was to paint later in Tahiti.

1890 was a period of waiting and reflection marked by some fine watercolours in which the drawing is at once ornamental and taut and by a multiform decorative production witnessed by a number of works which remained, all unknown, for a great many years in the possession of Marie Henry and her heirs. Among them was a set of gouaches with simplified, powerful accents that only reached the auction rooms a short time ago.

After his return to Paris in November 1890 Gauguin's one idea was to leave for the tropics. He had been obsessed with it for months. "The day will come (and perhaps soon)," he wrote to his wife, "when I can escape to the woods on a South Sea island and live there in ecstasy, peace and art." A sale of his works held in February 1891 brought in enough money to pay for the voyage and he embarked for Tahiti on April 4. In Paris, during the winter, he had spent a lot of time with the Symbolist group of writers, who welcomed him to the Café Voltaire, and he made friends with painters like Carrière and Redon who were connected with the movement.

Tahitian Eve

About 1892. Watercolour. 40 × 32 cm.
Musée de Peinture et de Sculpture, Grenoble.

We have already seen the cowering, woeful Eve of Gauguin's Breton period. After several intermediate essays, Gauguin discovered in Tahiti the exotic, primitive Eve he had dreamt of, standing upright in her naked beauty. He fixed her image under two chief aspects—before and after the Fall—with which he busied himself repeatedly. Here, in a paradisiac environment, is Eve before the Fall: "A fantastic garden offers its tempting blooms to the desire of an Edenic Eve who timidly stretches out her hand to pluck the flower of evil while the red wings of the Chimaera flutter whispering on her temples" (A. Delaroche, *D'un point de vue esthétique, à propos du peintre Paul Gauguin,* quoted by Gauguin in *Avant et Après,* 1903). More will be said about the image of Eve after the Fall in the following commentary.

The wanton posture of Eve's ripe body and the harmonious movement of her arms were inspired by a Javanese bas-relief from Borobudur, a photograph of which Gauguin had brought with him to Tahiti. The prototype of the figure appears, but with a different, not yet Tahitian, face, in an oil of 1890. It was repeated in Tahiti in a painting in the Ohara Art Museum, Kurashiki, *Te Nave Nave Fenua* (*Delightful Land*), and a woodcut of the same title as well as in several drawings of about the same period—two in charcoal where the figure is depicted in the same posture, one signed and dated 1892, and three watercolours in which figure and landscape are reversed; the third in *Noa Noa,* page 69.

The Devil's Words (Eve)

About 1892. Pastel on paper. 77 × 35.5 cm.
Signed, lower right: P. Gauguin.
Print Room of the Öffentliche Kunstsammlung, Basel.

The preceding plate shows us Eve before the Fall. Here we see, as described by Gauguin in the appendix to *Noa Noa*, "Eve after the Fall, still able to walk naked without shame, possessing all her animal beauty as on the first day ... Like Eve, her body has remained animal. But her head has evolved, her mind has learned subtlety, love has impressed an ironic smile upon her lips, and naïvely she searches her memory for the *why* of the present time. Enigmatically she looks at you."

This massive naked figure appears almost identical, with the same expressive gesture of the hands, in the composition dated 1892 *Parau Na Te Varua Ino* (*The Devil's Words*) (National Gallery, Washington); but there the demoniac apparition in the background (idol or ghost) is depicted fullface instead of in profile. It is viewed again in profile as here (whereas the nude figure is recumbent) in a masterpiece of similar inspiration, also dated 1892, the famous *Manao Tupapau* (*Spirit of the Dead Watching*), in the Museum of Modern Art, New York. A charcoal drawing of the nude figure alone was pasted on page 51 of *Noa Noa*. The same figure of Eve, reversed and with a different background, is also found in a monotype and a woodcut executed during Gauguin's second stay in Tahiti. A proof of the woodcut is attached to page 4 of *Noa Noa*.

There is a curious combination of the two characteristic postures of Eve before and after the Fall in two pictures painted during Gauguin's last years—one, dated 1898 and entitled *Te Pape Nave Nave* (*Delightful Water*) (The Leigh B. Block Collection, Chicago), for which there exists a preparatory study in charcoal; the other, dated 1902, *Adam and Eve* (Ordrupgaardsamlingen, Copenhagen). It is also worth mentioning at least one drawing, *Adam and Eve*, where the figure of Eve is quite unrelated to either of the two types we have considered.

Cows in a Landscape

About 1890. Watercolour. 26.4 × 31.9 cm.
Signed, lower left: P. GO.
Private Collection, USA.

Though it has no direct link with any of them, this splendid watercolour recalls several pictures painted in 1889 where cows and Breton peasants are depicted in the same peaceful arrangement and the same decorative style. The horizon is of enhanced, and the sky of diminished, importance, so that the plane surfaces glow with quality. The trunks of the willows with their lopped branches provide a fantastic backdrop and recall the cows' horn-crowned muzzles, whose curious forms they stress and multiply. Though taut, the drawing is bent into ornamental curves which forecast the "modern style." Trees, beasts and the peasant woman are imbued with the same vegetative tranquillity.

In an article published in the review *L'Œil* (July-August 1959), Maurice Malingue mentions the discovery, among the chattels left by the children of Marie Henry who kept the inn at Le Pouldu, of twenty-two photographs taken in 1895. He describes these photographs, which represent works Gauguin did at Le Pouldu 1889-1890, maintaining their original numbering. No. 18, an unpublished painting on pasteboard 28 × 32.5 cm. entitled *Cows and Peasant Woman in a Sunken Lane*, described as "a peasant woman viewed from the back, flanked by two cows one of which viewed from the front; in the background a landscape," might be connected with this watercolour.

Mimi and Her Cat

1890. Gouache on pasteboard. 17.6 × 16 cm.
Present whereabouts unknown.

In summer 1889, exasperated by the tourist crowds, Gauguin left Pont-Aven and took refuge in the isolated seaside village of Le Pouldu together with his faithful and generous friend, Meyer de Haan. They put up at the little inn kept by Marie Henry, called Marie Poupée, where, according to the guest-book, Gauguin lodged from October 2, 1889, to November 7, 1890. There he received frequent visits from his Pont-Aven pupils who helped him to decorate the entire main room of the inn, window-panes and ceiling included.

In 1924 Marie Henry (Madame Motheré) divided what mementos of Gauguin and the other Le Pouldu painters she still possessed between her two daughters, Ida (Madame Cochennec), daughter of Meyer de Haan, and Léa (Mimi), the offspring of an earlier affair. Léa's estate, from which this gouache comes, was auctioned off at the Hôtel Drouot, Paris, on March 16, 1959. There is a portrait by Meyer de Haan, *Marie Henry Nursing her Daughter Léa* (Private Collection, Lausanne), in which the figure of the child, a few months younger than here but very similar in its vivid treatment, would seem to suggest that Gauguin lent a hand.

Gauguin's notebooks are full of sketches of children and cats. It was during his stay at Le Pouldu that he most frequently employed gouache, a medium in which his friend and pupil Charles Filiger, who joined him there in July 1890, specialized.

In Paris, during that winter of 1890-1891, he drew a caricature of Moréas and etched a portrait of Mallarmé who presided over a dinner in his honour. He also composed a frontispiece for Rachilde's *Théâtre*. But he concentrated chiefly on an oil painting literary in inspiration and mannerist in execution which he bluntly entitled *Loss of Virginity*. It depicts his young mistress Juliette Huet lying open-eyed and stark naked in a Breton landscape; a fox, "the Indian symbol of perversity," seated by her side has laid his corrupting paw on her left breast. Jean Rotonchamp described it as "a virgin stricken to the heart by the demon of lewdness." A large drawing in black chalk on yellow paper, a study for the model's bust and the fox, belonged to Octave Mirbeau who had published a sensational article in the *Echo de Paris* to pave the way for Gauguin's exhibition and sale.

Young Girl with a Fox

1890-1891. Black chalk on yellow paper. 31.3 × 32.5 cm. Signed, upper left: P. Gauguin.
Mrs. Marcia R. Hirschfeld Collection, New York.

Gauguin returned to Paris from Brittany in November 1890 and stayed there till he left for Tahiti on April 4, 1891, associating with the group of Symbolist writers and poets who used to meet at the Café Voltaire. During that period and under that literary influence—probably early in 1891, as suggested by Rotonchamp who wrote a detailed commentary on the work—he painted a picture of quite transparent symbolism which he bluntly entitled *Loss of Virginity* (*The Awakening of Spring*) (Chrysler Art Museum, Norfolk, Virginia). It represents a naked girl lying open-eyed in the throes of desire in a Breton land-scape. By her side is a fox with one forepaw resting on her left breast. "A virgin stricken to the heart by the demon of lewdness," Rotonchamp called it. The fox, which Gauguin had practised drawing since 1888 (cf. pp. 194-197 of *Le Carnet de Paul Gauguin*, published by René Huyghe in 1952), reappears several times in his œuvre and always with the same demoniac sexual significance. Particularly in the wood carving of November 1899, *Soyez amoureuses, vous serez heureuses* (Museum of Fine Arts, Boston) where, as Gauguin himself explained to Emile Bernard, it represents the "Indian symbol of perversity."

The girl, seen here only from the waist up, was not a professional model but a twenty-year-old milliner's apprentice, not at all pretty but very expressive, named Juliette Huet. She was introduced to Gauguin by Daniel de Monfreid and became his mistress. When he left for Tahiti she was with child; he kept in touch with her and they met again on his return in 1893, but at that time he preferred "Annah la Javanaise." Juliette is believed to have died at a ripe old age about 1935 after destroying all her papers and mementos of Gauguin.

This drawing was part of the Octave Mirbeau sale (Galerie Durand-Ruel, Paris, February 24, 1919, No. 18) under the erroneous title of *The Girl with the Dog*. No doubt Gauguin had given it to the famous author and critic whom he met in January 1891 and who, at the request of Pissarro and Mallarmé, published in *L'Echo de Paris* of February 18, 1891, an impassioned appeal on behalf of the artist who was on the point of going into voluntary exile in Tahiti. The treatment of the nude figure was obviously influenced by Manet's *Olympia*—a picture which Gauguin greatly admired and made a copy of about that time, when it was hung in the Luxembourg Museum, Paris, in 1890.

Te Faruru
(To Make Love)

1892. Gouache. 43.5 × 20.5 cm.
The Museum of Fine Arts, Springfield, Massachusetts.

In June 1891 Gauguin landed in Tahiti where, as in Brittany, he spent some months in a phase of acclimatation, meditating, observing and drawing. "Till now," he wrote on November 7 to his new friend Daniel de Monfreid, "I have done nothing of any importance; I am quite content to search within myself, and not in nature, to learn to draw a little, for drawing is all that really counts—I am also collecting documents to paint in Paris." On March 11, 1892, he wrote to him again: "I am working more and more, but so far only studies or rather documents that are piling up." To his wife he wrote at the same time: "I am working hard and I think that when I come back I shall have enough documents in my pocket to paint for a long time." Like Delacroix in Morocco —at Arosa's he must have seen several of the marvellous watercolours done on that trip—his first thought was to collect on the spot an exotic "documentation" to be utilized later in France— sketches after nature which fanciful dreamers rely on more than they admit and which Watteau called his "thoughts." A quantity of drawings, watercolours and monotypes come from a file that Gauguin had marked: *Documents, Tahiti, 1891–1892–1893*. Many of those sheets, intended as illustrations for some manuscript or other, had been cut out with scissors; in others the pencil drawing on the obverse reappears as if printed on the reverse. Gauguin had a limited repertory of forms and occasionally did a drawing with his sheet of paper resting on a metal or earthenware plate coated with brown ink. In this way he obtained a sort of reversal or monotype which enabled him to see how a figure looked best and to use it facing different ways in different compositions.

The *Carnet de Tahiti*, edited by Bernard Dorival in 1954 and since dismembered, sheds an important new light on Gauguin's life and method of work during his first stay in the South Seas. It reveals him in his most intimate and spontaneous vein. The 401 drawings in black and white or heightened and the six watercolours differ in subject matter and in value; the best jostle the worst and original accents lie cheek by jowl with mechanical repetitions. Many are rapid jottings of silhouettes and gestures, or more careful studies of faces viewed from front or side, rarely at a three-quarter angle, caught to the life for the sake of their ethnic type or characteristic expression. Gauguin's instinct led him to generalize and immobilize his figures, but he was quite capable of noting in a sketch a peculiar pose or dynamic gesture. The *Carnet* also contains many drawings of animals, but landscapes are few and summarily treated and still lifes almost entirely lacking. Gauguin was less interested in nature or inanimate objects than in the human figure whose mystery and plastic dignity he rediscovered, not indeed in its anatomical structure but as rhythm and arabesque.

In July 1892 he wrote to his wife: "I am hard at work; now I know the ground and its fragrance and the Tahitians, though I render them in a very enigmatic fashion, are nonetheless Maoris and not Orientals from the Batignolles... I have done thirty-two canvases so far... quite a lot of drawings and sketches, a few sculptured trifles." In that same exaltation of his creative faculties Gauguin drew the *Crouching Tahitian Girl*, the incarnation of

Head of a Woman

About 1891-1892. Pencil and watercolour.
17 × 11 cm.
Alex M. Lewyt Collection, New York.

This watercolour drawing adorned the front of page 11—on the back were three figure sketches and a bird study—of *Carnet de Tahiti* now dismembered but published in facsimile in 1954 with a scholarly introduction by Bernard Dorival. It was a small volume of 130 leaves measuring 17 × 11 cm. of which twenty-nine were blank and the others covered with innumerable sketches in black and white or heightened and with watercolours; they date from Gauguin's first stay in Tahiti and reveal the most intimate and spontaneous aspect of his activity as a draughtsman. Most of the drawings are sketches of silhouettes and gestures or studies of heads jotted down, like this one, for the sake of their strange ethnic type or characteristic expression. This mysterious, exotic face with its wide steady eyes, enveloped in a red shawl held in place by the dignified gesture of the hand, recalls similar notations made by Delacroix in Morocco which Gauguin admired and some of which he may have seen at the home of his guardian Gustave Arosa.

Maori beauty and a counterpart to *L'Arlésienne* in its linear perfection and symbolic value. Tehura, the model, was the lovely wahine who shared the artist's pandanus-thatched cabin. She is also portrayed as *Eve* before and after the Fall, naked and erect "in all her animal beauty as on the first day," her contorted posture inspired by the bas-reliefs at Borobudur.

But Gauguin was not content to be at one with "all nature" and the Maoris whose language he learned to speak and whose customs he adopted. In his art he recreated the lost myths of Tahiti and attempted to recover something that no longer existed—the secrets that even the natives themselves had forgotten. In fact, sixty years had passed since 1831 when, "in the silence of the dark nights," the last *harepo* or high priest on the point of death had disclosed the traditional sacred hymn of Polynesia to an American consul named J.A. Moerenhout who published it in his *Voyage aux Iles du Grand Océan* in 1837. Gauguin transcribed it textually in his

Crouching Tahitian Girl

About 1892. Pencil, charcoal and pastel.
55.3 × 47.8 cm.
The Art Institute of Chicago.

This figure, one of Gauguin's most perfect works, is deservedly famous for it combines in a sovereign rhythm modelling in the round with the decorative harmony of the picture plane. The girl embodies the magnificent beauty of the Maoris celebrated by Victor Segalen in his *Hommage à Gauguin*: "Handsome athletes with happy muscles, harmonious in dynamic repose, with joints more supple than sinewy, a face with well set nose neatly outlined by the brush stroke; ...prominent eyes, ...full, blood-blue lips, ...the Maori woman, whether in motion or stooping, draws an unbroken line from shoulder to fingertips.

The volume of the arm is very elegantly turned..." (Preface to *Lettres à Daniel de Monfreid*, 1918.)

This sheet is the squared study for the central figure of the picture *Nafea Faa Ipoipo* (*When are we getting married?*) dated 1892 and now in the Öffentliche Kunstsammlung, Basel. The same figure, in the same squatting posture, appears in a *Tahitian Landscape* of 1891 and in several other works, among them *E Haera Oe I Hia* (*Where are you going?*) dated 1892 (Staatsgalerie, Stuttgart), *Ea Haere Ia Oe*, a variant of the same theme in 1893 (Hermitage, Leningrad), and *Te Fare Hymene* (*The House of Songs*) also dated 1892 (Meadows Collection, Dallas).

Other preparatory drawings of the same figure, either alone or in a group, are extant. On the back of the sheet reproduced here is a charcoal sketch of another Tahitian girl.

manuscript *Ancien Culte Mahorie* which was written in 1892–1893 and, as René Huyghe proved in his introduction to the facsimile edition of 1951, constitutes the source and key of *Noa Noa*. This document is illustrated by splendid watercolours which accompany the text and bring back to life the Maori pantheon as Gauguin saw it with the help of Polynesian *tikis* (stylized figures engraved in stone or on the handles of tools) and the decorated fabrics called *tapas*. The first of these illustrations shows us, viewed from the side, the *Sacred Couple*—the supreme god *Taaroa* and one of the series of wives who bore him the other gods and the elements. Several watercolours depicting idols or divinities, some of them terrifying,

The Sacred Couple—The God Taaroa and One of His Wives

1892-1893. Watercolour. 21.5 × 17 cm.
Musée du Louvre, Paris.

This sheet is page 7 of the manuscript of *Ancien Culte Mahorie* acquired by the Louvre in 1927 with the whole Moreau-Nélaton Collection. The precious notebook, composed during Gauguin's first stay in Tahiti in 1892-1893, consists of 38 leaves measuring 21.5 × 17 cm. but only 57 pages are used; on its cover, in Tahitian fibre, are the signature *PGO* and the title *Ancien Culte Mahorie*. A facsimile edition was published in Paris in 1951 with a masterly introduction by René Huyghe telling how it came to be written and demonstrating its significance as the source and key to *Noa Noa*.

Gauguin derived his knowledge mainly from a bulky work in two volumes, *Voyage aux Iles du Grand Océan* (Paris 1837), by

J.A. Moerenhout, one-time American Consul in Tahiti in whom the last high-priest, on his deathbed, had confided the secrets of the age-old religion of Polynesia.

This watercolour, the first in the manuscript, depicts in profile the supreme god *Taaroa*, creator and principle of the universe, and one of the series of wives who bore him the other gods and the elements. Their bodies are adorned with ritual tattooing in a dark blue pigment extracted from the burnt kernel of the tiaïri. The geometrical stylization of figures and backdrop is directly inspired by the *tikis* of the South Sea Islands. Gauguin made tracings of these designs, which are engraved on stone or on the handles of implements, and pasted them, heightened with watercolour, on pages 168 and 169 of the manuscript of *Noa Noa*. The four lines of text at the top of the page are the close of the story of the creation transcribed in Maori; the French translation is given in the following chapter of the manuscript.

Maoti tau te ori ori
Atou te' marama ora toura
Ta hina pohé' a toura
Ta Te'fatou o té' taata.

belong to this same religious cycle, which Gauguin developed at the same time in his oils. When he crossed the island alone and climbed the sacred mountain on whose summit had stood the *Marae*, a temple where human sacrifices were once offered, surrounded by a skull-topped fence, he discovered *The Mysterious Water*; the life-giving spring gushes out of the rock and towards it leans a silhouetted figure that comes straight from an Egyptian tomb.

Between Brittany and Tahiti Gauguin's style did not undergo a complete transformation but merely a harmonious development. There is now a different environment and greater technical facility; primitive man has replaced the peasant and nature has become a paradise. The line has lost its rigid, angular character and the aggressive tension that often marks the birth of an art; it has grown wavy and supple as a liana. The rather forced predominance of Japanese prints and folk arts has been superseded by the influence of Egypt, India and Polynesia, of Raphael and the pre-Renaissance Italian painters, of Ingres and Manet, sometimes even of Puvis de Chavannes.

Bathers Under a Tree

About 1891-1892. Pen and watercolour. 24.7 × 31.7 cm. Inscribed above: "Le ciel est par-dessus le toit... Verlaine."
Private Collection, Basel.

Men and women bathing under the decorative spreading tree, branched like a candelabrum, which appears again and again in Gauguin's work during this period. The composition of this drawing, so delicately washed with watercolours, is based on a very complex system of volutes and dotted lines drawn in pen. Though there is no direct link, it may be connected with the oil dated 1892 *Fatata Te Miti (Near the Sea)* in the National Gallery of Art, Washington, and also with the watercolour on page 37 of the manuscript of *Ancien Culte Mahorie* and page 79 of *Noa Noa*.

The poem transcribed above the picture, the last stanza of which is also copied in *Avant et Après*, is one of the best known in Paul Verlaine's *Sagesse* (1881). Gauguin met Verlaine during the winter of 1890-1891 at the meetings of the Symbolists in the Café Voltaire. A performance given for their joint benefit at Paul Fort's Théâtre d'Art on May 27, 1891, was not a success.

Le Ciel est, par dessus le toit
Si Bleu, si Calme!
Un arbre, par dessus le toit
Berce sa Palme.

La Cloche dans le Ciel qu'on voit
Doucement tinte.
Un oiseau sur l'arbre qu'on voit
Chante sa plainte.

Mon Dieu, mon Dieu, la vie est là
Simple et tranquille
Cette paisible rumeur là
Vient de la ville.

— Qu'as-tu fait, ô toi que voilà
Pleurant sans cesse,
Dis, qu'as tu fait, Toi que voilà.
De Ta Jeunesse?

Verlaine.

Parau Hanohano
(Fearful Words)

1892. Watercolour. 15.1 × 21.2 cm. Inscribed, lower left: Parau / hanohano *(Fearful Words). Signed, lower centre:* P. Go *with the remark* Opoi *(given). The Fogg Art Museum, Harvard University, Cambridge, Massachusetts.*

On his arrival in Tahiti in June 1891 Gauguin was welcomed by Paulin Jénot, a lieutenant of Marines, who had come to meet Captain Swaton, Gauguin's fellow-traveller from Numea. Jénot helped Gauguin over the material difficulty of settling at Papeete and the two men became close friends. To express his gratitude, Gauguin gave Jénot several paintings and drawings, among them this watercolour. Hence the word *Opoi*, after the signature, meaning "given". In an autograph note from Carnac (Brittany) dated June 6, 1939, Jénot states that it was painted in 1892 in his house at Papeete where Gauguin, who was living in the Mataiea district at the time, called on his way through. Jénot's memoirs, which give valuable information on Gauguin's life and work during his first stay in Tahiti, were published in the *Gazette des Beaux-Arts*, in a special number on Gauguin, January-April 1958, pp. 115-126.

There is an oil painting of the same title and probably done at the same time, but the composition is different. The tree with branches lopped off like those of a candlestick appears in several pictures painted in 1891 and 1892, for instance *Tahitian Pastorals* (Hermitage, Leningrad), *I Raro Te Oviri* (*Under the Pandanus*) (Minneapolis Institute of Art), *Mata Mua* (*In Olden Days*) (Private Collection, New York) and *Arearea* (*Amusement*) (Musée d'Orsay, Paris). The two idols with stylized faces are evidently linked with the cycle of *Ancien Culte Mahorie*.

Musique Barbare

1891-1893. Watercolour on silk. 12 × 21 cm.
Signed, lower right: PGO. Inscribed, lower
right: musique / Barbare.
Öffentliche Kunstsammlung, Basel.

The title of this forceful watercolour contains two words of which Gauguin was particularly fond. Indeed, he adopted and developed Delacroix's famous theory on the music of colour and never tired of extolling the value of everything "barbaric" or primitive and running down the decadence and corruption of civilization. Two of his most important paintings are entitled *Poèmes Barbares* (1896, Fogg Art Museum, Cambridge, Massachusetts) and *Contes Barbares* (1902, Museum Folkwang, Essen).

The violently coloured, magical figures that compose this "barbaric music" belong to the Maori pantheon which Gauguin brought back to life. On the left, between the two higher divinities, we can recognize the profile of the idol he often used during his first stay in Tahiti. Instead, the strange figures on the right are those of the Tikis, or inferior spirits, depicted in very similar shape on page 21 of *Ancien Culte Mahorie* and page 56 of *Noa Noa*.

The general atmosphere and certain details of this composition also recall the coloured woodcuts *L'Univers est créé* and *Te Atua* or *Les Dieux*. The last figure on the left reappears with the same geometrical stylization but different colours in the watercolour on page 14 of *Ancien Culte Mahorie* where there is an account of the Atuas.

In August 1893 Gauguin landed at Marseilles and in the following November organized an exhibition at Durand-Ruel's Paris gallery which, though sponsored by Degas, was a failure. A second auction of his works in February 1895 was only moderately successful and in March he bade farewell to Europe and set sail for the South Seas. But before that, in the summer of 1894, he went for the last time to Brittany where his peasant models were tinged by his memories of Tahiti. He took advantage of this stay in France to reproduce his most important drawings in a set of woodcuts which show extraordinary originality in technique and expression and to write, in collaboration with Charles Morice, *Noa Noa*, the legendary account of his voyage to Tahiti.

Pape Moe (Mysterious Water)

1893. Watercolour. 31.8 × 21.6 cm. Signed, lower right: PGO.
The Art Institute of Chicago.

An oil painting of the same subject inscribed *Pape Moe* (*Mysterious Water*) and dated 1893 appears as No. 4 in the Gauguin Exhibition organized by Durand-Ruel in November 1893 and is now in the Emil G. Bührle Foundation, Zurich. The same motif is repeated, reversed and with a few alterations, in a monotype in the Denis Rouart Collection, Paris, and in a wood-carving.

This is how Gauguin describes the scene in his account, in *Noa Noa*, of the excursion he made alone right across the island and to the top of the sacred mountain. "All of a sudden there was a sharp bend and I saw, standing erect against the rock wall which her two hands seemed rather to caress than to cling to, a young girl, naked: she was drinking at a spring that gushed out high up among the rocks." But no sooner had she sensed the presence of the "stranger" than she dived with a shriek of terror. "I rushed to the water's edge and gazed into its depths —not a soul to be seen; only a huge eel gliding among the pebbles on the bottom." In the plastic, pictorial transposition of the tale, the female apparition, symbol of the island's secret, has become a male figure inspired probably by the mural paintings in Egyptian tombs, photographs of which Gauguin used more than once in his own compositions.

Nave Nave Fenua
(Delightful Land)

About 1892. Colour woodcut. 35.5 × 20.5 cm.
National Museum, Stockholm.

Head of a Breton Girl

About 1894. Pencil, red and black crayon,
washed. 22.4 × 20 cm.
The Fogg Art Museum, Harvard University,
Cambridge, Massachusetts.

Its monumental simplicity and humanity make this one of Gauguin's finest drawings. The model was a Breton peasant girl of pensive mien and retiring disposition. Her slightly almond eyes gaze into the distance, bearing witness to the strong influence of oriental art in general and Japanese prints in particular. This drawing may possibly date from about 1889, as assumed by John Rewald—not without a question mark—and others, though the works of that period have a bolder and more decidedly "cloisonné" outline, and a starker strength. But it was more probably done about 1894.

On returning to France, Gauguin stayed in Brittany for the last time at Pont-Aven and Le Pouldu from April to November 1894. During those months his Breton subjects are coloured, as would seem to be the case here, by his memories of the South Seas. The flexibility of the line, the quality of the light, the easy fullness of the style, even the facial type, are marked by the experience of Tahiti.

Parahi Te Marae
(The Site of the Temple)

About 1892. Watercolour. 18.5 × 22.9 cm.
The Fogg Art Museum, Harvard Univer-
sity, Cambridge, Massachusetts.

A painting of the same subject dated
1892 (Mr. and Mrs. R. Meyer de
Schauensee Collection, Devon, Pennsyl-
vania) bears the inscription *Parahi Te
Maras* (*sic*)—There stands the Marae, the
temple of the primeval religion.

This strange, striking composition
represents the sacred mountain of the
ancient Maori cult, of which Charles
Morice gives the following description
in his introduction to *Noa Noa*: "It is the
top of the mountain, the inaccessible
spot that, in past ages, only the feet of the
gods might touch ... A site of horror
and sublimity; starkness of funereal rites;
invisible but obvious signs of the grim
ancient worship. There, no doubt, human sacrifices were once offered. The
painter has preserved their trace in the
rigid fence on which—as sculptured wit-
nesses, vague but all the more terrifying
for their imprecision—human skulls are
impaled."

In the oil painting for which this watercolour was the preliminary sketch, the
fence with the death's heads that limits
the sacred enclosure overshadowed by
the profile of the mysterious idol has a
different shape which is directly inspired
by carved bone native ornaments often
drawn by Gauguin.

The famous manuscript of *Noa Noa* is extant in two versions; the original remained in the hands of Charles Morice, while the second and final one, now in the Louvre, was recast by Gauguin and enriched with numerous drawings and documents. We reproduce some of the watercolours, often mentioned and executed at different times, that illustrate it. One is the *Flowers* on the dust-cover, justifying the title *Noa Noa*, which means "fragrance"; another the remarkable *Woman with a Mango*, of which Degas owned the version in oils; still another a lush *Tahitian Landscape* that Gauguin utilized for the background of one of his last pictures, painted in the Marquesas Islands.

During his second stay in Tahiti Gauguin, now quite at home there, felt less urge to draw and, when the wretched state of his health allowed, preferred to paint or sculpt directly. In 1896, a year that was no less fruitful than 1892 had been, he painted his South Sea Venus, *The Queen of Beauty*, a superlative work which, though different, can bear comparison with the *Venus* of Giorgione or Manet's *Olympia*. The watercolour of the same subject might be either a preliminary sketch or a replica. As so often in such cases, it is hard to say which. Now curves tend to disappear and are outbalanced by straight lines, vertical and horizontal, which emphasize the monumental quality of the figures. "Figures are what I prefer," Gauguin wrote in July 1900. It was about that time that he did the striking pastel, *Tahitian Woman*, which conciliates in its magnificent rhythm the fullness of volume that haunted Gauguin's memory and the majestic mural arrangement to which his genius aspired, "imposing those ancestral forms with so decisive a gesture that I defy any painter who paints in future in Tahiti not to be dominated to the point of exasperation and sterility by the obsessive mastery of Gauguin's drawing" (Victor Segalen, *Hommage à Gauguin*, 1918 and 1950).

Manuscript of *Noa Noa*
(Journey to Tahiti)

1893-1894. 31 × 23 cm.
From page 64 to page 73, all illustrations come from the manuscript of *Noa Noa*.
Cabinet des Dessins, Musée du Louvre, Paris. RF 7259.

Flowers
Watercolour.

This superb watercolour of flowers adorns the page immediately preceding the numbered pages in the manuscript of *Noa Noa* as the very symbol of the title which, in Maori, means "fragrance."

The manuscript, which Daniel de Monfreid presented to the Louvre in 1925, is a thick in-folio volume containing 182 leaves measuring 31 × 23 cm. The pages, numbered from 1 to 345, are written in black or blue ink and illustrated with 59 watercolours and coloured woodcuts, 18 woodcuts in black and white, a great many photographs and other documents. This is not the original version but a later recast compiled during Gauguin's second stay on Tahiti. *Noa Noa* proper, viz. the section in praise of Tahiti, the scented isle, ends on page 204 and dates from 1895-1896 (though the illustrations, many of which were cut out and pasted in, may be earlier or later). The bases for a critical study were outlined by René Huyghe in 1951 in his introduction to *Ancien Culte Mahorie*, another of Gauguin's illustrated manuscripts which constitutes the key to *Noa Noa*.

Flower pictures by Gauguin are rather rare. The most numerous and best date from his second stay in the South Seas and were perhaps painted under the influence of Odilon Redon who had a special liking for them and whose first successes were admired by Gauguin before leaving Europe for the last time. In July 1900 he wrote to the connoisseur Emmanuel Bibesco: "You speak of painted flowers, but I really do not know which you mean though I paint so few: that is because (as you have noticed, no doubt) I am not a painter from nature—today still less than formerly... And then, this is not really the land of flowers."

Vahine No Te Vi
(Woman with a Mango)
Watercolour.

Page 63 of the manuscript of *Noa Noa* in the Louvre is illustrated by three unrelated watercolours. The one in the middle is obviously a replica, but only from the waist up and in a slightly different posture, of the admirable figure painted in 1892, *Vahine No Te Vi* (*Woman with a Mango*), a masterpiece acquired by Degas at the sale of Gauguin's works on February 18, 1895 (Cat. No. 2)

and now in the Baltimore Museum of Art, in the room devoted to the Etta Cone Collection which also contains a large number of pictures by Matisse.

The topmost of the three watercolours depicts the black sow abandoned by a brother of the god Oro and her seven piglets; it is also found, together with the text of the relative legend, on page 27 of the manuscript of *Ancien Culte Mahorie*. The third, at the foot of the page, is an indoor scene connected with the painting of 1892, *Te Fare Hymene* (*The House of Songs*), which belongs to the Meadows Collection (Dallas).

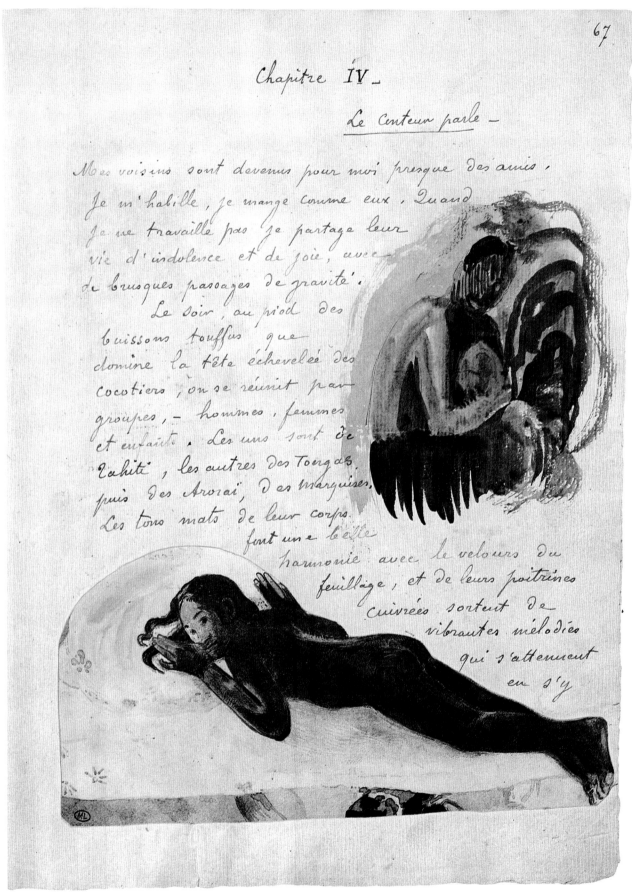

Chapitre IV_

Le Conteur parle_

Mes voisins sont devenus pour moi presque des amis.
Je m'habille, je mange comme eux. Quand
je ne travaille pas je partage leur
vie d'indolence et de joie, avec
de brusques passages de gravité.

Le soir, au pied des
buissons touffus que
domine la tête échevelée des
cocotiers, on se réunit par
groupes, — hommes, femmes
et enfants. Les uns sont de
Tahiti, les autres des Tongas,
puis des Aroraï, des Marquises.
Les tons mats de leur corps
font une belle
harmonie avec le velours du
feuillage, et de leurs poitrines
cuivrées sortent de
vibrantes mélodies
qui s'atténuent
en s'y

The Storyteller Speaks

Watercolour.

66

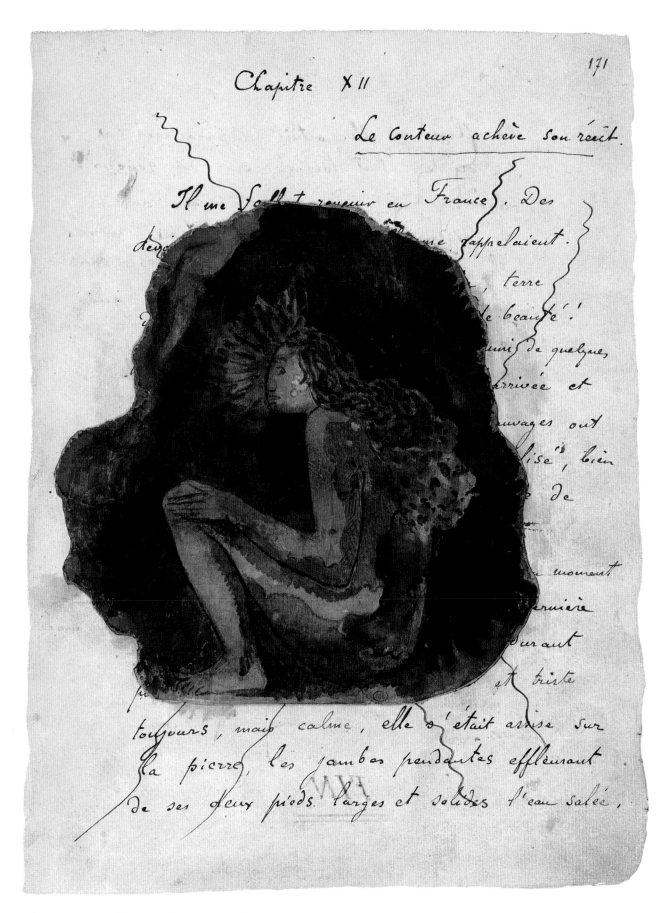

Chapitre XII

Le Conteur achève son récit.

The Storyteller Ends His Tale
Watercolour.

Tahitian Landscape

Watercolour.

Nothing could give a better idea of the magnificent scenery of the South Sea Islands than this fine watercolour which was perhaps done from nature and then cut out and pasted on page 179 of the manuscript of *Noa Noa* at present in the Louvre. "Wanting to suggest a wild and luxuriant nature," Gauguin wrote in the appendix to *Noa Noa*, "a tropical sun that makes everything around it blaze, I had perforce to give my figures an appropriate setting ... Hence all these fabulous colours, this fiery yet soft and muted air."

Gauguin used this landscape, transposed to his ultimate, iridescent key loaded with pinks and purples, for the background of one of his last pictures, *Women and a White Horse* (Museum of Fine Arts, Boston) painted a few weeks before his death, in March 1903.

Wahine Walking

Watercolour.

69

Landscape

Watercolour.

Landscape

Watercolour.

Copulation

Watercolour.

The Idol Hina

Colour woodcut.

Tahitian Woman

1891-1893. Pastel and gouache. 40 × 31 cm.
The Metropolitan Museum of Art, New York.

Te Arii Vahine
(Queen of Beauty)

1896. Watercolour. 17.2 × 22.9 cm. Signed, lower left: PG. *Inscribed, lower centre:* TE ARII VA[HI]NE.
Private Collection, New York.

A study for (or after) the famous canvas of the same title, dated 1896, in the Hermitage, Leningrad.

This is how Gauguin described the composition, in April 1896, in a letter to Daniel de Monfreid illustrated with a sketch heightened with watercolour. "A nude queen reclining on a green lawn, a servant girl picking fruit, two old men by the big tree arguing about the tree of knowledge, in the background the sea; this rapid, shaky sketch will only give you a vague idea. I think that in colour I have never done anything with such a grand, solemn resonance. The trees are in bloom, the dog keeps watch, on the right two doves coo."

Here we are shown the South Sea Venus in her paradisiac environment, her primeval beauty enhanced by the majestic linear rhythm—note how the melody of the oblique lines is measured by the verticals—and the rich, deep colour. The red fan behind her head is a token of ancient lineage, while the tropical fruits in the foreground justify the popular title—The Woman with the Mangoes.

This splendid figure, which rivals yet differs from Giorgione's *Venus* and Manet's *Olympia*, is repeated several times in Gauguin's work. For instance, (reversed) in the pen drawing dated 1903 that illustrates page 121 of the manuscript of *Avant et Après*, in two woodcuts, of which one inserted inside the front cover of *Noa Noa*, the other used as the heading of the journal *Le Sourire*; and in a woodcarving.

Whence Come We?
What Are We?
Whither Go We?

1898. Watercolour study on tracing paper squared in graphite. 205 × 375 cm. Signed and dated, lower left.
Musée des Arts Africains et Océaniens, Paris.

This faintly coloured drawing on squared paper is inscribed on the lower left: "De l'amitié dans le souvenir / cette pâle esquisse / Paul Gauguin – Tahiti 1898."

In a letter to Daniel de Monfreid, dated February of that same year, Gauguin emphasized the importance he attached to the large canvas he had painted in November-December 1897, *Whence Come We? What Are We? Whither Go We?* (Museum of Fine Arts, Boston), whose general composition is faithfully reflected in this watercolour.

The finished canvas may be taken as representing the artist's spiritual testament, painted at a time of intense work just before his attempted suicide late in 1897. In the letter to Monfreid of February 1898, he says:

"I must tell you that my resolution was quite taken for the month of December. So before dying I set out to paint a large canvas which I had in mind, and throughout the month I worked day and night in an unheard-of fever. Of course it is not a canvas made like a Puvis de Chavannes, with study after nature, then preparatory cartoon, etc. No, it is all tossed off without a model, from the tip of my brush, on an old piece of burlap full of knots and wrinkles, so that it looks terribly rough.

"It will be said that it's slipshod, not finished. It is true that one cannot well judge oneself, but nevertheless I believe that this canvas not only surpasses all the previous ones in value, but also that I'll never do a better one or another as good. I've put into it before dying all my energy, and such an aching passion in terrible circumstances, and so clear-cut a vision without corrections, that the hastiness disappears and life surges out of it. It doesn't reek of the model, the craft and the alleged rules —from which I have always held off, but sometimes with anxiety.

"It's a canvas 4.50 metres long by 1.70 in height. The two upper corners are chrome yellow with the inscription on the left and my signature on the right, like a fresco frayed at the corners and laid over a golden wall. On the lower right, a sleeping baby, then three crouching women. Two figures dressed in purple confide their thoughts to each other; a figure deliberately over-sized and crouching, despite the perspective, raises her arm in the air and looks in surprise at these two personages who dare to muse on their destiny. A figure in the middle plucks a fruit. Two cats beside a child. A white goat. The idol, both arms raised mysteriously and with rhythm, seems to point to the beyond. A crouching figure seems to be listening to the idol; then, lastly, an old woman beside the dead one seems to accept, to resign herself to what she is thinking and ends the legend; at her feet, a strange white bird holding a lizard in its paw represents the uselessness of vain words. It all takes place beside a wooded stream. At the back, the sea and the mountains of the neighbouring island. Despite the tonal transitions, the look of the landscape from one end to the other is constantly blue and Veronese green. Against it all the nude figures stand out in bold orange. If one were to say to the Beaux-Arts students competing for the Rome Prize, "The picture you have to do shall represent Whence Come We? What Are We? Whither Go We?", then what would they do?"

He wrote about it warmly to Daniel de Monfreid in March 1898; and again he commented on it at length and justified his work in a letter of March 1899 to André Fontainas, who had reproached him for too literary a conception, and also in a letter of July 1901 to Charles Morice.

Nearly all the symbolic figures brought together in this immense synthesis, and clearly recognizable in this watercolour sketch, were taken over from previous pictures of his and used again in subsequent ones.

◁ Arearea No Varua Ino
(The Amusement
of the Evil Spirit)

About 1894. Watercolour. 24.3 × 16.5 cm.
National Gallery of Art, Washington, D.C.

Crouching Woman,
from behind

About 1902. Monotype. 48.3 × 29.3 cm.
Mr. Eugene V. Thaw Collection,
New York.

79

Tahitian Woman

About 1900. Pastel. 56 × 49.6 cm. Signed, upper left: PGO.
The Brooklyn Museum, Brooklyn, New York.

By cleverly inventing new methods of his own, Degas completely renovated the style and technique of the pastel which, after 1880, became more and more his favourite medium. Odilon Redon also used it frequently, especially after 1890, and drew from it rich, mysterious resonances. Following in the footsteps of these two artists whom he admired without reserve, Gauguin has here further developed the chromatic potentialities of the pastel; but his monumental conception evokes rather the simplicity and clarity of fresco painting than the hatchings or the powdery dryness of coloured chalks.

This grandiose figure of a Tahitian woman, viewed from close up, forcefully modelled yet entirely in the picture plane, placed off centre and balanced by the decorative palm leaf on the right, is imbued with terrific primeval energy. It clearly calls for the spaciousness of mural painting, which was the real vocation of Gauguin's genius but which he was not destined to fulfil. Form, balance and colour scheme have caused this work to be ascribed to 1900 or thereabouts. In July of that year Gauguin told Emmanuel Bibesco, in the letter already quoted: "Figures are my real love."

In July 1901 Gauguin sought still more distant and freer lands, the Marquesas Islands, where he died on May 8, 1903. He chose Dominique, the largest and most beautiful, settling in the little village of Atuana where, in a coconut palm grove on the seashore, he built a cabin he called the House of Joy. "Here," he said, "poetry arises spontaneously and one only has to let oneself dream while painting to suggest it." Now coloured woodcuts, more and more simplified and "barbaric," took up most of his time. His last set of drawings, interspersed with monotypes, illustrates his ultimate manuscript, *Avant et Après*, which was finished in February 1903. It tells of an extremely violent storm that all but submerged the cabin he had just built. "My house destroyed with all my drawings, material accumulated in twenty years. It would have been my ruin." When Gauguin died, a few months later, it was not nature but the indifference and hostility of his fellow men that brought about the loss of that treasure whose value we can only guess. Police and missionaries, with whom Gauguin had been at loggerheads, were particularly set against the caricatures and drawings they considered "obscene" and which must have been very numerous. He too may have desired the disappearance of those personal documents, which he had not intended for publication. He had written in *Avant et Après*: "A critic comes to see my paintings and asks, with bated breath, for my drawings. My drawings! Oh, no! They are my private letters, my secrets." But in this field too he had shown enough during his lifetime for us to judge his merits. The most enthusiastic and qualified admirer of Gauguin's drawings was undoubtedly Degas, who had bought several at the 1895 sale where no less than thirty-five were exhibited beside forty-six paintings.

Two Marquesan Women

About 1902. Monotype heightened with colours.
37.2 × 32.5 cm.
The Philadelphia Museum of Art.

BIOGRAPHY AND BACKGROUND

LIST OF ILLUSTRATIONS

BIOGRAPHY AND BACKGROUND

1848 **Birth of Paul Gauguin in Paris, June 7. His father Clovis Gauguin is an editor on the staff of the opposition newspaper *Le National*. His mother, née Aline Chazal, is the daughter of the socialist and feminist militant Flora Tristan (1803-1844), who was of Peruvian ancestry.**

1849 **August: The family sails from Le Havre for Peru. Gauguin's father dies of a ruptured artery on board ship in the Straits of Magellan and is buried in Chile. Aline Gauguin and her two children Paul and Marie (born 1847) sail on to Lima, where they are taken in by Aline's uncle Don Pío de Tristan Moscoso.**

> 1851 December revolution in Paris: Napoleon III founds the Second Empire (1852-1870).

1854–1855 **Return to France, settling in Orléans, where Clovis Gauguin's father and uncle live.**

> 1856 Eugène Boudin makes the acquaintance of young Claude Monet at Le Havre and guides his early efforts.

1859 **Paul continues his schooling at the Saint-Mesmin Seminary in Orléans.**

> 1859 Monet and Pissarro meet in Paris. Birth of Seurat.

> 1861 Manet exhibits for the first time at the Paris Salon, and meets Baudelaire. Cézanne arrives in Paris to study art.

1862 **Paul rejoins his mother in Paris, where she had settled the year before as a seamstress. He prepares for the entrance examination at the Naval Academy.**

> 1862 Monet, Renoir and Sisley meet in Paris at Gleyre's studio. Degas paints his first racecourse pictures at Longchamp.

> 1863 Salon des Refusés, where Manet's pictures, especially the *Déjeuner sur l'Herbe*, cause an uproar. Death of Delacroix.

> 1864 Pissarro exhibits at the Salon. Birth of Toulouse-Lautrec at Albi.

1865 **Aline Gauguin appoints Gustave Arosa, a well-known collector and family friend, as legal guardian of her children. Too old to enter the Naval Academy, Paul joins the merchant marine as a cadet and sails for Rio de Janeiro, a voyage lasting three months.**

> 1865 Manet exhibits *Olympia* at the Salon.

1866 **Second voyage to Rio. Then, in October, he sails from Le Havre as second lieutenant on board *Le Chili*, on a thirteen-month voyage round the world.**

> 1866 Renoir and Sisley paint together at Marlotte (Forest of Fontainebleau).

1867 Death of his mother, the news reaching him when his ship calls at a port in India. Back to Le Havre with *Le Chili* in December.

> 1867 Paris World's Fair. Extreme severity of the Salon jury: all the future Impressionists are rejected, except Degas. Death of Baudelaire and Ingres. Birth of Pierre Bonnard.

1868–1869 Transferring to the French Navy, he is assigned to the *Jérôme-Napoléon*, cruising the Mediterranean and the Black Sea. Coming of age in 1869, he (together with his sister Marie) inherits money and property in Orléans from his mother and his paternal grandfather. Voyages in the Mediterranean on board the *Jérôme-Napoléon*.

> 1869 Renoir and Monet work at Bougival: the Impressionist technique takes form. Birth of Matisse.

1870 During the Franco-Prussian War he serves in the North Sea, where his ship captures four German ships.

> 1870 After the French defeat, proclamation of the Third Republic.

1871 Released from war service, he gives up the sea and settles in Paris.

> 1871 Paris convulsed by the Commune (March-May). Birth of Rouault.

1872 Through his guardian Gustave Arosa, Gauguin enters the Paris stockbroking office of Paul Bertin, at 11 Rue Laffitte, where he meets Emile Schuffenecker, an amateur painter. In the autumn he meets a Danish girl, Mette Gad (born 1850), staying in a Paris pension run by friends of the Arosa family.

1873 November 22: Marriage of Paul Gauguin and Mette Gad. They live at 28 Place Saint-Georges, 9th arrondissement.

1874 August 31: Birth of his son Emile.
Paints as an amateur and begins building up a collection of Impressionist pictures (Manet, Cézanne, Pissarro, Renoir, Monet, Sisley).

> 1874 First group exhibition of the Impressionists, Paris, Boulevard des Capucines, on Nadar's premises.

> 1875 First Impressionist sale at the Hôtel Drouot auction rooms in Paris.

1876 A landscape of his, *Sous-bois à Viroflay (Seine-et-Oise)*, is accepted at the Salon. At the end of the year, gives up his stockbroking job with Paul Bertin. His first meeting with Pissarro probably dates from this year.

> 1876 Second group exhibition of the Impressionists.

1877 Moves with his family to 74 Rue des Fourneaux (Vaugirard), where his landlord, the sculptor Bouillot, initiates him into sculpture.
December 25: Birth of his daughter Aline.

1877 Third Impressionist exhibition. Cézanne works with Pissarro at Pontoise.

1878 Paris World's Fair. Théodore Duret publishes *Les Peintres impressionnistes.*

1879 Employed by the banker André Bourdon at 21 Rue Le Peletier. Invited at the last minute to take part in the fourth Impressionist exhibition (so that his name does not figure in the catalogue); he lends three Pissarros for the exhibition. Evenings at the Café de la Nouvelle-Athènes, where he rubs shoulders with Manet, Degas, Renoir, Pissarro, Edmond Duranty, George Moore.
May 10: Birth of his son Clovis.

1879 Odilon Redon publishes his album of lithographs *Dans le rêve.*

1880 Shows at the fifth Impressionist exhibition with seven paintings and one bust. Employed now by an insurance company.

1881 Shows at the sixth Impressionist exhibition with eight paintings and two sculptures. J.K. Huysmans describes his landscapes as "watered down Pissarro" but praises a nude study. The Impressionists' dealer Paul Durand-Ruel buys three of his canvases for 1,500 francs; and he himself buys a Manet seascape and a Jongkind.
April 12: Birth of his fourth child Jean-René.

1881 Birth of Picasso.

1882 Shows eleven paintings, one pastel and one sculpture at the seventh Impressionist exhibition. Stock market crash and financial crisis in Paris. His own finances are precarious, as he hesitates between business and art. Visits to Pissarro at Pontoise and Osny.

1883 Seeks employment with the art dealer Georges Petit.
December 6: Birth of his son Pola.

1883 Death of Manet and Gustave Arosa.

1884 Moves with his family to Rouen for eight months. Trip to Southern France where he copies Delacroix's *La Mulâtresse* in the Musée Fabre, Montpellier. Badly in need of money, he takes a job with a Roubaix tarpaulin factory, as their representative in Denmark, whither his wife returns with the children in October. He joins them in November, bringing his collection with him: it will stay in Denmark. Mette gives French lessons to earn some money.

1884 Salon des Indépendants founded in Paris by Seurat, Signac, Cross and Redon.

1885 Exhibition at the Copenhagen Society of the Friends of Art, considered scandalous and soon closed down. Leaving his wife in Denmark, he returns to Paris with his son Clovis. In dire need, he works as a bill-sticker, then as an administrative secretary for the French railways.

1885 Pissarro meets Theo van Gogh, then Signac and Seurat, and adopts the Pointillist technique in 1886. Vincent van Gogh painting at Nuenen.

1886 Takes part in the eighth and last Impressionist exhibition with nineteen paintings and a wood relief. Sells a painting to the painter and etcher Félix Bracquemond, who puts him in touch with the ceramist Ernest Chaplet. To Brittany in June, staying at the Gloanec Inn at Pont-Aven, where he meets Emile Bernard and Charles Laval. Back in Paris in November, where he meets Vincent van Gogh.

1886 Impressionist exhibition organized in New York by Durand-Ruel. In Paris Félix Fénéon publishes *Les Impressionnistes en 1886*. Revelation of the Douanier Rousseau at the Salon des Indépendants. Publication of Rimbaud's *Illuminations*.

1887 In Paris until April, when his wife pays him a visit, and on the 10th he leaves with Charles Laval for Panama "to live as a savage." From there they soon move on to Martinique, where Gauguin paints several landscapes prefiguring his Tahitian pictures. Back in Paris in November, prostrate with fever and dysentery. Lives with Schuffenecker at 29 Rue Boulard.

1887 Birth of Juan Gris and Marc Chagall. Mallarmé publishes his *Poésies complètes*.

1888 February-October: At Pont-Aven in Brittany with Meyer de Haan, Charles Laval and Emile Bernard. Out of their common work and discussions come "Synthetism" and "Cloisonnism," a style of painting of great importance for the twentieth century. Theo van Gogh organizes Gauguin's first one-man show at the Boussod and Valadon Gallery, Paris. On October 21 he leaves Pont-Aven for Arles, where he joins Vincent van Gogh at the latter's invitation. They live together for two months, but their relations are strained from the start. On December 24, after a quarrel, Van Gogh in a fit of madness cuts off part of his own ear. Gauguin hurries back to Paris, again staying with Schuffenecker.

1888 Bonnard, Vuillard, Maurice Denis, Ranson and Sérusier meet at the Académie Julian, Paris. Cézanne makes a long stay in Paris. The Belgian painter James Ensor paints *The Entrance of Christ into Brussels*.

1889 During the Paris World's Fair, Gauguin and Schuffenecker organize an exhibition of the "Impressionist and Synthetist Group" at the Café des Arts, with the backing of the proprietor, M. Volpini. The young Nabis, Sérusier, Maurice Denis and Bonnard are much impressed by it.
Third stay in Brittany, the longest and most decisive. Summer at Pont-Aven in the inn run by Marie-Jeanne Gloanec. In October he moves to Le Pouldu, to the inn of Marie Henry, where he is joined by some of his cronies, Séguin, Filiger and Meyer de Haan.

> 1889 Construction of the Eiffel Tower for the Paris World's Fair. Verlaine publishes *Parallèlement*, and Bergson *Les Données immédiates de la Conscience*. Van Gogh, suffering from intermittent fits of madness, enters the Saint-Rémy asylum, near Arles.

1890 Returns to Paris from Brittany in November. Homeless, he again stays with Schuffenecker in the Rue Boulard.

> 1890 The literary magazine *Le Mercure de France* is launched by Alfred Vallette. Bonnard, Vuillard, Denis and Lugné-Poe share a studio in Montmartre, 28 Place Pigalle. Van Gogh settles at Auvers-sur-Oise, near Paris, May 21, and there commits suicide, July 29. Munch's first stay in Paris.

1891 Gauguin associates with the Symbolist writers who forgather each week at the Café Voltaire. Copies Manet's *Olympia*. Resolves to go to Tahiti.
February 23: First sale of 30 pictures at the Drouot auction rooms (catalogue prefaced by Octave Mirbeau) to raise the money for his voyage.
March 23: Farewell banquet in his honour at the Café Voltaire.
April 4: Sails for Tahiti.
First stay in Tahiti (June 1891-July 1893): Landing at Papeete on June 8, Gauguin is disgusted by the European colony at the capital and acquires a native hut in the Mataiea district, some 25 miles south of Papeete.

> 1891 Van Gogh Retrospective Exhibition at the Indépendants. Death of Seurat. The Natanson brothers launch the *Revue Blanche*. Gatherings of Symbolist poets at the Café Voltaire, Place de l'Odéon. Aurier's Manifesto of Symbolist Painting in the *Mercure de France*. Bonnard exhibits for the first time at the Indépendants. Lautrec draws his first poster for the Moulin Rouge. First exhibition of the Nabis.

1892 A fruitful year of work for Gauguin, despite ill-health.

> 1892 Matisse arrives in Paris and enrolls at the Académie Julian. Lautrec's first colour lithographs. Seurat retrospective exhibition at the *Revue Blanche*.

1893 At the end of his tether, a sick man, Gauguin is compelled to return to Europe.

Paris-Brittany (August 1893 – February 1895). Goes to Orléans to collect the inheritance of his uncle Isidore, then rents a studio in Paris where he lives with Annah the Javanese.

November 4: Opening day of his exhibition at Durand-Ruel's; though no financial success, it has much influence on Bonnard, Vuillard and the other Nabis.

1893 Opening of the Vollard Gallery in Paris. Matisse and Rouault meet in Gustave Moreau's studio. First exhibition of the Munich Secession group.

1894 January: Goes to Copenhagen (last meeting with his wife).

April-December: At Pont-Aven and Le Pouldu with Annah.

December: Returns to Paris. Annah has disappeared, after looting his studio.

1894 Caillebotte bequest to the Musée du Luxembourg, Paris. Odilon Redon exhibition at Durand-Ruel's.

1895 Gauguin decides to go back to Tahiti.

February 18: Second auction-sale at the Hôtel Drouot, catalogue prefaced by a letter from Strindberg. Sale a complete failure.

Second stay in Tahiti (July 1895 – September 1901): Settles on the west coast in the Punoauia district.

1895 Cézanne exhibition at the Vollard Gallery. First public motion-picture shows given by the Lumière brothers. Publication of Rimbaud's *Poésies complètes*, with a preface by Verlaine.

1896 Gauguin's health is breaking up and he suffers from a sense of being alone and an outcast. However, in November he writes: "I am recovering and, thanks to this, have got through a lot of work."

1896 Alfred Jarry's *Ubu Roi* performed at the Théâtre de l'Œuvre. Matisse's first appearance at the Salon de la Nationale. Death of Verlaine. Marcel Proust publishes *Les Plaisirs et les Jours*. Kandinsky and Jawlensky arrive in Munich from Russia.

1897 Death in Copenhagen of Gauguin's daughter Aline. Stops writing to his wife. Stays a while in hospital. A year of masterpieces: *Nevermore, Whence come we?* The *Revue Blanche* publishes his manuscript *Noa Noa*.

1897 Munch makes a long stay in Paris, doing lithographs and woodcuts which show Gauguin's influence.

1898 **After an attempt to commit suicide, Gauguin takes a clerk's job in the Public Works office at Papeete.**

1898 Death of Mallarmé. Paul Klee studies at Knirr's in Munich.

1899 **Continually in trouble with the local authorities. Publishes the satirical broadsheet *Le Sourire*.**

1899 Group exhibition of the Nabis at Durand-Ruel's in homage to Odilon Redon. Matisse, Derain, Jean Puy and Laprade meet at the Académie Carrière. Signac publishes *D'Eugène Delacroix au Néo-Impressionnisme*. Death of Sisley.

1900 Paris World's Fair. Seurat retrospective exhibition organized by Félix Fénéon. Picasso's first stay in Paris.

1901 **August: "I'm off for the Marquesas. At last!" (letter to Daniel de Monfreid). Settles at Dominica in September.**

1901 Death of Toulouse-Lautrec at the Château de Malromé. Apollinaire comes to Paris. Odilon Redon exhibition at Vollard's. Van Gogh exhibition at Bernheim-Jeune's. Derain introduces Vlaminck to Matisse at the Van Gogh exhibition; Matisse visits Derain and Vlaminck at Chatou.

1902 **August: Gauguin's heart is giving him trouble and his legs are covered with open sores, causing him intense suffering. He realizes he is mortally ill and thinks of returning to France for treatment, but Monfreid advises him against it.**

1902 Matisse exhibits at Berthe Weill's, as does Picasso. In Munich Kandinsky opens his own art school and becomes chairman of the Phalanx group.

1903 **March: contentions with the local government, the Bishop and the police (for championing the natives). Unjustly sentenced on March 31 to three months' imprisonment and a fine of 1,000 francs. He is too poor to go to Tahiti to lodge an appeal.**
April: Gauguin's last letter to Daniel de Monfreid ends: "All these worries are killing me."
May 8: Death of Paul Gauguin.

1903 Rouault helps to found the Salon d'Automne, seconded by Matisse, Marquet and Bonnard. Death of Pissarro and Whistler. Matisse, Dufy, Friesz and Marquet exhibit at the Salon des Indépendants. Matisse, Puy, Manguin and Marquet exhibit at Berthe Weill's, but the word "Fauve" had not yet been coined. Gauguin Memorial Exhibition at the Salon d'Automne. In Berlin works by Bonnard, Cézanne, Gauguin, Van Gogh and Munch are exhibited by the Secession.

LIST OF ILLUSTRATIONS

SKIRA

PRINTED BY
IRL IMPRIMERIES RÉUNIES LAUSANNE S.A.

0290   PRINTED IN SWITZERLAND